NEW JERSEY

ASK6

LANGUAGE ARTS LITERACY TEST

MaryBeth Byrouty, M.Ed.

George Washington Middle School

Wayne, New Jersey

BARRON'S

About the Author

MaryBeth Byrouty has taught sixth-grade language arts for four years at George Washington Middle School in Wayne, New Jersey. She has served on several curriculum committees that integrated the district's writing and reading programs, aligned these programs with the New Jersey Core Curriculum Content Standards, and developed thematic language arts and social studies units. She has attended several NJ ASK language arts workshops and was asked to be a turnkey trainer for colleagues. Prior to teaching at George Washington, MaryBeth taught language arts, math, science, and social studies to fifth graders for seven years.

All inquiries should be addressed to:
Barron's Educational Series, Inc.
250 Wireless Blvd.
Hauppauge, NY 11788
www.barronseduc.com

ISBN-13: 978-0-7641-3942-0
ISBN-10: 0-7641-3942-8

International Standard Serial Number: 1942-0811

Printed in the United States of America
9 8 7 6 5 4 3 2 1

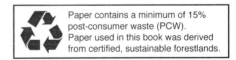

Paper contains a minimum of 15% post-consumer waste (PCW). Paper used in this book was derived from certified, sustainable forestlands.

CONTENTS

INTRODUCTION

What do you as a student look forward to during your sixth-grade year? Dances? Maybe. Field trips? Usually. Spending time with friends? Definitely. Taking the language arts standardized test? Probably not. Why is this the case? Well, after preparing for months, you are expected to remember everything you have learned. The fact is, this test is a way to show what you know. Teachers and parents also tell you that the test is important, you should give your best effort, and you should keep going even when you feel your brain cannot possibly think anymore. WOW! This is easier said than done, right? Is there a magic potion that you can buy and then, poof, the stress goes away? Sadly, there isn't; however, there is this book!

This book has been written for you, the sixth-grade student. It cannot promise to make all of the stress magically go away, but the tips and practice exercises can help to increase your confidence. Confidence is one of the keys to performing better on the NJ ASK6 Language Arts Literacy test. As you flip through the pages, this book will take you through everything you will need to know about the test.

You might be wondering why you even have to take this test in the first place. You also may be wondering what kinds of questions will be on the test. Well, this book gives you the answers to these two questions and more. By the time you are done working with it, you will have learned about the major parts of the NJ ASK: the persuasive essay, speculative writing prompts, picture prompts, and multiple-choice and open-ended questions based on reading passages. These chapters will tell you about each section of the test and even give you examples so that you can practice what you have learned. The last chapter provides you with two sample timed tests to give you the best practice possible. Don't worry; the answers are provided too so you can check how well you have done. Now there is only one thing left to do. Let's get started!

Chapter 1

NJ ASK OVERVIEW

I t's springtime, the weather is beginning to get nicer, students get to enjoy recess outside again, and everyone seems to be in a better mood. That mood quickly changes when your teacher makes the statement that few students want to hear: "The NJ ASK test is coming up soon." Immediately after the groans, the panic begins to set in. Why in the world does the state of New Jersey make students take this test? In this chapter you will get the answer to that question and probably many others that you may have about the test.

In this chapter you will:

- get an explanation of the NJ ASK Grade 6 Language Arts Literacy test

- find out about the parts of the test

- learn how the test is scored

- discover how to best prepare yourself for the test

EXPLANATION OF THE TEST

First of all, the state of New Jersey is not making you take a test to punish you, drive you crazy, or see how much stress you can handle. Instead, it has another reason. That reason is to see how well you can show that you understand the Core Curriculum Standards. These standards are skills and concepts that the state believes you should know at the end of every grade. Basically, it's the information you should have learned and should know by the end of sixth grade. Each grade level must take a standardized test like the NJ ASK (New Jersey Assessment of Skills and Knowledge). A standardized test is one in which many students take the same test and then the test is scored in the same way. Sixth-grade students must take the NJ ASK for math and language arts. All of these tests are put together by teachers, administrators, and a publishing company. This book will concentrate only on preparing you to take the language arts test.

PARTS OF THE TEST

You may now be asking, "Well, what's on the language arts test?" This part of the NJ ASK is given on two days and has four ways to assess what you know:

1. reading passages and answering multiple-choice questions,

2. reading passages and answering open-ended questions,

3. writing a story from a speculative prompt,

4. writing a persuasive essay from a prompt.

Each of these areas will be covered in a chapter of this book. First you will have to write a persuasive essay that expresses your opinion on a topic and why everyone should agree with you. Then you will have to read fiction and non-fiction stories, and answer questions based on each story. Some of the multiple-choice questions will ask you about the main ideas and details of the story, the author's point of view, and the setting of the story. Others may ask you about the vocabulary words used in the story, or about the characters that you just read about. The open-ended questions will usually ask for your opinion about a detail in the story, and then ask you to support your answer with facts from the story.

Can this book give you the exact questions on the test so you can memorize the answers? Sorry, but the answer is no. No one is allowed to see the test before the testing date—not even your parents or teachers. Once the test is opened, even teachers aren't allowed to view what is on it. The test is secured, which means that only the publishers know exactly which questions are on it. If the tests were shown to everyone, then the state would have to make a new test every year, and that would be too expensive. What we do know is the *types* of questions that are on the test. We can use these similar questions to help prepare you for the test.

HOW THE TEST IS SCORED

Some students may also be asking, "What happens if I fail the test? Will I have to repeat sixth grade?" The good news is you really can't fail this test. It is not the kind of test where you can get a 100% or a 25%. In fact, you probably won't get every single question perfectly correct. Your job is to do the best you can and earn as many points as you can. You can do this by answering the questions to the best of your ability. Each correctly answered question earns you points.

On the language arts test, the points are added up to get a final score. A score of 200–249 means you have scored proficiently. A proficient score means you have shown that you have learned and now understand the skills and ideas that you need by this point in school. If your score is 250 or higher, you have scored in the advanced proficient range. Advanced proficient means that you have learned the skills and concepts you need, and you are also able to demonstrate more knowledge or skills in language arts. Finally, if your score is under 200, you are partially proficient. This doesn't mean you have failed. What it means is that you have learned some concepts and skills, but you need some help in learning other skills or concepts that you will need by the end of sixth grade. Usually if this is the case, you will take a class to help you better understand what you may be confused about on the test.

DO YOUR BEST

Now, everyone should try really hard to concentrate while they are taking the NJ ASK. This can be really difficult, especially if you get nervous, or you begin to get tired. Remember to keep going, because the results will be worth it. Most students will do this. However, there are some students who either guess on everything, don't care about their answers, or think about what they will be doing on the weekend instead of concentrating on the test and their answers. There are other students who give up and just write anything when they get too tired or nervous. The important thing to remember is to try your best so that the results are accurate and really show what you know.

Your teachers and principal will look at the results of the NJ ASK and think that this is how much you have learned during sixth grade. No matter which range you score into, it should really prove what you understand. Students who score in the partially proficient range may have to take a class to make sure they understand all of the sixth grade material. This class can be a big help to some students. However, if you just give up on the test and then wind up having to take a class where the teacher tells you everything you already know, you will be bored and wish you had tried harder during the week of testing. Try to remember that when your brain is tired and you don't feel like concentrating anymore. You can do it, but you have to prepare!

PREPARING FOR THE TEST

So, should you just sit back and wait for the testing to begin? No! There are many things you can do to prepare yourself for the NJ ASK. The first thing you can do is to read this book carefully, complete all of the practice exercises, and remember the tips so that you can feel confident on testing days. Keep in mind, by the time you finish this book, you will be ready to take the test. You will have all of the tools to do well!

Here is a list of all the things you can do to prepare for testing:

What You Can Do	How?
Practice	■ Do your best when you complete the practice exercises in this book. ■ Review the answers carefully. If you answered correctly, congratulate yourself! If not, read the explanations carefully and go back to see where you went wrong. Don't get discouraged. Learn from your mistakes!
Be Mentally Prepared	■ Get a good night's sleep the night before testing so that you are wide awake and ready to concentrate. ■ Eat a good breakfast on the morning of a testing day to make sure you have energy. You will also be able to concentrate more on the test if you don't have to concentrate on your stomach growling.
Remember and Relax	■ Listen to your teacher's advice and remember what you have learned. Your teacher has given you the tools to do well. ■ Take a deep breath if you get very nervous. Some nerves may be good, but being too nervous can stop you from concentrating on the test. Remind yourself that you are prepared for this test. You have completed this book and are ready to do a great job!

THE PERSUASIVE ESSAY

One section of the Language Arts NJ ASK is the persuasive essay. In this section you will be given a writing prompt and then you will be asked to reply by giving your opinion. The essay will have to be completed in approximately 45 minutes. Sounds easy, right? Well, it can be, but you have to **respond with a complete essay**. Not sure what a complete essay is? Don't worry. By the end of this chapter you will be!

In this chapter you will:

- learn what it means to write persuasively

- find out the proper format for the persuasive essay

- evaluate a persuasive essay using the NJ Registered Holistic Scoring Rubric

- write and evaluate your own five-paragraph persuasive essay

WRITING PERSUASIVELY

When you have a disagreement with someone, do you like to be right? Of course you do! Most people want others to see things their way. Well, when you write a persuasive essay, you get to prove to someone that your opinion is the right one, and explain why they should agree with you. On the NJ ASK, you will have to write a persuasive essay. First, let's talk about what is expected from you in this essay. Your job will be to read the writing prompt that you are given and write an essay that not only states your opinion, but also *persuades* the reader to agree with you.

What does it mean to persuade someone? When you are asked to do this, your goal is to get them to see things your way. In other words, you have to get the reader to agree with you. It means to write in a way so that you provide the reader with information that supports your opinion, and then details to support the information. That way, when the reader is done reading your essay, he or she will think, "Wow, this author is right. I never thought of things that way!"

When you have to write a persuasive essay, keep three things in mind:

1. Make sure you state your opinion clearly.

2. Give the best three reasons why a reader should agree with you.

3. Use your best writing techniques.

You want to keep these things in mind because there will be a person who will evaluate, or score, your essay. This person will score you on a scale of 1–6, six being the best score. We will talk more about scoring later in this chapter.

THE WRITING PROMPT

Now, let's discuss the type of writing prompts you may be given. It's easy to have an opinion about things like your favorite sports team or your favorite singer. However, chances are you will not be asked about these topics. Instead, the topic is usually school-related. You might be asked for your opinion on:

- school uniforms

- extended school year

- choices in the lunchroom

No matter what the topic is, make sure you read the writing prompt carefully and understand what it is asking you to do. For instance, read the following writing prompt: *The board of education in your town has just voted to require all students to wear uniforms. Do you agree with the board's decision?*

For this prompt, you have to write an essay stating whether or not you agree that all students in your town should wear school uniforms. However, you cannot simply stop there; you must give three reasons why you feel a certain way about school uniforms. Persuasive essays for the NJ ASK should always include *three* reasons that support your opinion.

When reading a writing prompt, keep these ideas in mind:

- Reread the question a few times to make sure you understand what it means.

- It helps to write down what the question means, or list what it is asking for, in the brainstorming section of your booklet.

- It even can be wise to write down what it might NOT be asking.

Here is another example: *Due to budget cuts, the board of education in your town has decided to discontinue all after-school activities. Write a letter to the board of education members telling them how you feel about their decision.*

In order to respond to this prompt correctly, you have to consider two parts of the question. First, decide how you feel about the topic: eliminating after-school activities. Second, you must remember to write your response in *letter form*, and not just the typical essay format. Basically, if the question asks for you to write a letter, make sure you respond with one. Make a note of this on your brainstorming page!

BRAINSTORMING

Once you have read the prompt and understand what you are supposed to do, what is the next step in answering the question? Many students would probably say the next step is to begin writing their essay. WAIT! There is a very important step that comes before writing the essay! This step is **brainstorming**. Before you begin to write, take about five minutes to brainstorm your ideas. Many students don't think this step is important, but it is. Taking the time to brainstorm can help you get many of your ideas down on paper, and these ideas can help you organize your essay later. There are many ways to brainstorm ideas. The one thing they all have in common is that they have you write down what comes to mind when you think about a certain topic. One style of brainstorming is called webbing and another is called listing.

Here are the two brainstorming methods and an explanation of each:

Method	Explanation
Webbing	■ Write the topic inside a circle. ■ Then write down the words or ideas that come into your mind when you think of this topic. ■ Draw a circle around the words and then draw a line from those circles to the center circle. ■ Write down words or ideas that now come to mind. ■ Draw a circle around these words and connect them to the web.
Listing	■ List your topic. ■ Under the topic, write down all of the ideas that come into your head when you think about that topic.

You should brainstorm for about five minutes. Since you don't have an unlimited amount of time to write the whole essay, using about five, but no more than ten, minutes to brainstorm should give you time to think of some good ideas. If you do not feel comfortable with the brainstorming techniques you have read about here, and instead have another method that you feel comfortable with, it's okay to use your own method. The important thing is that you do some type of brainstorming. Here is an example of a writing prompt and two types of brainstorming:

Writing Prompt: *Bullying has been a problem in many schools. Bullies single out students for dressing, thinking, and acting differently from the general group. To eliminate some of this bullying, the board of education in your town has just voted to require all students to wear uniforms so that they will be dressed similarly. Do you agree with the board's decision? Why or why not?*

Your brainstorming might look something like this:

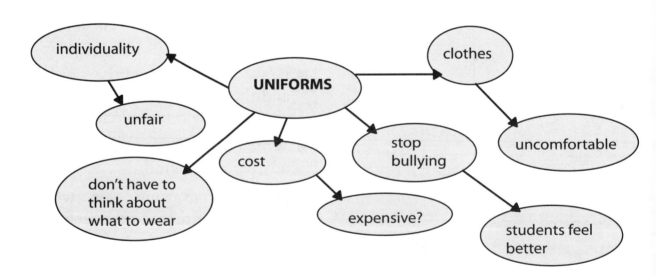

Or this:

Uniforms

- are unfair
- clothes
- Are they expensive?
- uncomfortable
- student individuality
- don't have to think about what to wear
- It might stop bullying.
- Students feel better if they don't get picked on.

Now it's your turn to try brainstorming. After you finish reading the writing prompt below, make sure you understand what the question is asking, then brainstorm ideas in the space provided. Use the type of brainstorming with which you feel most comfortable. Remember, take about five minutes to brainstorm. If you run out of things to write after only a minute or two, don't give up. Rest your brain for a second, and then try again. You will be surprised how many ideas you can think of if you give yourself the chance!

Writing Prompt: *Students often forget much of what they have learned the previous year over the summer months. This is called summer loss. Many teachers are complaining that they must review many concepts that were previously taught to the students before they can move on to the current year's material. This causes them to lose time, and therefore they may not finish teaching what needs to be covered by June. In order to prevent this loss, people have proposed that the school year be extended through the summer months. What would you say to the people who have made the proposal?*

Brainstorm here:

Time to Check:

Did you:

- reread the question to make sure you understood what it was asking?

- write down what the question means?

- brainstorm for about five minutes, or did you immediately stop after you couldn't think of any more ideas?

It's important to keep thinking and not give up. You never know which ideas will help you to write an excellent persuasive essay!

FORMING AN OPINION

Now that you have some ideas to include in your essay, you can begin to write it. First, think of how you feel about the writing prompt. Do you agree or disagree? Why? On this test, you cannot be for <u>and</u> against a topic.

You must choose *one* side and attempt to get your reader to agree with you. There is no in between, so choose carefully. You can use a T-chart like the one below to help you organize your ideas either for or against the topic, so that you know where you stand. Under the Pros side, list all of the reasons you agree with the topic. On the Cons side, list the reasons you might disagree with the topic. Here is an example of a T-chart for the school uniform topic:

PROS	CONS
1. Students wouldn't have to think about what to wear.	1. They are not comfortable.
	2. They might cost a lot.
2. No one would get made fun of because they don't wear the latest fashion.	3. They take away a student's individuality.

Now it's your turn. Try filling in this T-chart for the extended school year writing prompt that you just read. Then take a look at both sides and see which you agree with more.

PROS	CONS

You have decided on your opinion. It's now time to decide how you want to persuade your readers to agree with you. You can appeal to their emotions. This is their sense of heart, or their beliefs. Try to make the reader *feel* a certain way. For example, you can make the reader feel badly for students who have to wear uniforms that hold back their individuality. Or instead, you can appeal to the logical side of your readers. This is the side that makes *sense* to them. Something makes sense to your reader because you have given them many statistics to support your opinion, and therefore they must agree with you because common sense tells them you are right.

Once you have decided how you want to approach the persuasive essay, think of three reasons why your opinion is correct. As you think about the topic, look back at your brainstorming ideas to help you. You don't need to use all of the ideas, just the ones that you feel are important. Once you have your three reasons, put them in order *ending* with the one you feel is your strongest reason. Can you guess why you end with the strongest reason? If you answered because that is what the reader reads last and remembers most, you are right! Make that last reason worth remembering! As you write down each reason, next to it also write down a few words telling a bit more about the reason. You will be adding details to explain your reason. Again, use your brainstorming ideas to help you. You will refer to this list as you write your essay.

It's your turn again! Write your ideas below.

Your opinion:

_____

_____

_____

_____

Your three reasons and details:

1. _____

   _____

2. _____

   _____

3. _____

   _____

WRITING THE ESSAY

Let's move onto the essay. It should be five paragraphs altogether. The first paragraph should include your introduction, then general information about the topic, followed by your *thesis*. You may have never heard of a thesis before. The thesis is your opinion, or how you feel about the topic. The second paragraph should consist of the first reason that supports your thesis, and details and examples that support the first reason. The third paragraph should consist of the second reason that supports your thesis, and details and examples that support the second reason. The fourth paragraph should consist of the third reason that supports your thesis, and details and examples that support the third reason. The last paragraph is your conclusion. You briefly restate your thesis and sum up your essay.

Here is an outline of what your persuasive essay should look like:

Paragraph 1: introduction, information, thesis
Paragraph 2: reason 1, details, examples
Paragraph 3: reason 2, details, examples
Paragraph 4: reason 3, details, examples
Paragraph 5: thesis, summary of essay (conclusion)

The First Paragraph

Let's work on paragraph one first. The first sentence or two of your introduction should be interesting enough to hook the reader. That is why we call it the hook, or *lead*. It should make the reader want to read the rest of the essay. It should NOT be your thesis. Not sure how to begin your essay? Well, there are several possible ways to begin.

These are some ways to begin your essay, followed by examples related to the school uniforms writing prompt:

Types of Hooks	Examples
Ask a question of your reader.	How can students show their individuality?
State an interesting bit of information about the topic.	Students love to show off their individuality by wearing different types of clothing.
Write three words describing your topic.	Unfair, boring, and ugly are three words to describe how students feel about school uniforms.
Have the reader think about something.	Imagine going to a school where everyone looks the same; the same clothes, the same colors, the same patterns.

After your hook, add two or three more sentences to the paragraph that tell about the topic, but do not state your thesis or any reasons to support your thesis. Think of **other** interesting details that tell about your topic. You can include other examples or statistics that you know about the topic here. After you add those details, you can write your thesis. The thesis should be the *last sentence* of your first paragraph.

Note: When you write your thesis, try not to use the words *I think.* These words should be kept out of your entire essay. They make your essay sound too personal. If you decide to use first person (words including *I, we, us*), follow with a stronger word than *think.* For example: I urge you, I request, I challenge.

The goal of the essay is to make readers agree with you, not because you say so or because you are bullying them into believing it, but because you have presented the facts or ideas in such a way that they almost *have* to agree with you. You don't want to write your essay so that you sound like an angry bully; instead, you should sound like a lawyer arguing a case. Imagine if a lawyer got up and said to the jury, "Ladies and gentlemen, my client is innocent and you'd better agree because I say so, and if you don't, you are stupid!" What do you think the jury would do? Most likely they would not listen to anything else the lawyer has to say, and the lawyer would lose the case. You don't want to make the same mistake. So leave out "I think" and bully comments and use your best vocabulary to impress the reader!

Vocabulary Counts

Speaking of vocabulary, the persuasive essay is the place to use the best words that you know. Remember, you have a limited amount of time to write your essay. Most students will not be able to write an entire rough draft, and then edit, revise, and rewrite a final copy in that time. Use your best vocabulary and writing style from the beginning, so that you have less revising to do. This means using strong verbs and quality, descriptive words. Only use them if you know their meaning. Trying to use a word because it sounds important, but makes no sense, will only confuse the reader and probably lower your score.

For example, "Students should not *have to* wear school uniforms." The sentence is correct, but it could use a stronger, more persuasive word. Here's another try: "Students should not be *mandatory* to wear school uniforms." This sentence has a problem too. The writer used an action word that has a similar meaning to the words *have to,* and it sounds more persuasive, but it is used incorrectly. This makes the writing confusing to the reader.

This is a better sentence: Students should not be *required* to wear school uniforms. The word *required* is a stronger vocabulary word, and it also is used correctly in the sentence.

Remember two things when choosing vocabulary words:

1. Check to see if you are using words that are too easy and boring. If so, use better or more descriptive words.

2. Remember that if you aren't sure about whether your new word is the correct choice, it probably is not a good choice. You don't want to confuse the reader. Choose a new word only if you are sure it really improves your sentence.

Here's what a proper thesis might look like for our writing prompt on school uniforms: *Students should not be required to wear school uniforms.* Okay, now let's put together paragraph one. Below is an example for the topic of school uniforms.

Imagine going to a school where everyone looks the same: the same clothes, the same colors, the same patterns. Sounds pretty boring, right? Well, that is something that might happen in our town if some people have their way.

No one wants to be bored in school, whether it is by teachers or by what people wear. Therefore, students should not be required to wear school uniforms.

Now it is your turn to write paragraph one for the extended school year writing prompt on page 11. Remember the parts of the paragraph and their order: hook, interesting information, and then thesis. Write your first paragraph on the lines below, remembering to write neatly so that the reader can understand what you have written.

_____

_____

_____

_____

_____

_____

_____

_____

Time to Check:

Did you:

- begin with an interesting hook?

- end with your thesis?

- leave out the phrase "I think" and bully statements?

- remember to indent the first line of your paragraph?

- remember to write neatly?

Make sure you fix anything you missed!

The Body of the Essay

Paragraphs two, three, and four are all set up similarly to each other. First, you must include a transition word. Transition words help take the reader from one part of the essay to another. Since you are stating reasons that give more information about your thesis in these paragraphs, use an additional signal transition word to begin each paragraph.

Some additional signal transition words are:

first of all	initially	the third reason
secondly	also	next
thirdly	in addition	lastly
then	another	additionally

Begin paragraph two with a transition word, followed by a comma. Then state the first reason people should agree with your thesis. Follow this sentence with other sentences that tell more about your reason. Here is where you can give specific data, examples, or other pieces of information related to the reason. You can use additional signal transition words within your paragraphs if you are listing the details in order.

Set up paragraphs three and four the same way: transition word, reason, and details. However, the fourth paragraph should include your *strongest* reason. You want to leave readers thinking that you must be right since the last reason was so convincing.

Following the first paragraph below are paragraphs two, three, and four for our school uniform topic:

Imagine going to a school where everyone looks the same: the same clothes, the same colors, the same patterns. Sounds pretty boring, right? Well, that is something that might happen in our town if some people have their way. No one wants to be bored in school, whether it is by teachers or by what people wear. Therefore, students should not be required to wear school uniforms.

First, school uniforms can be very uncomfortable. They aren't made from the nicest fabrics and can be itchy and rough on skin. If students aren't comfortable in their clothes, they can become distracted and have trouble listening to the teacher and learning lessons. This could affect their grades in a negative way. Then students would be worried about their grades, and have another reason for not being able to concentrate in class.

Secondly, school uniforms may cost a lot of money. Parents may not be able to afford the cost of the uniform. If they can buy any type of clothes for their kids, then they can shop in places they can afford. They can even wait for the clothes to go on sale, or use store coupons. It isn't fair to force parents to pay more money than they have to for clothes.

Thirdly, students show their individuality through their clothes. Clothing is a way to express how you feel, or what interests you have, such as a sports team like the Yankees. Students need to have a way to express themselves. Clothing is one of those ways. Some people may get picked on by bullies for expressing themselves in a different way, but that isn't always true. The bullies will just find something else to make fun of about someone if everyone is dressed the same. Uniforms would take away one way to be an individual.

Now it's your turn. Continue your essay that you began on page 19 for the extended school year by writing paragraphs two, three, and four on the lines that follow.

_____

_____

_____

_____

_____

Time to Check:

Did you:

- begin each paragraph with a transition word, followed by a comma?

- list one reason that supports your thesis in each paragraph?

- remember to save the strongest reason for your fourth paragraph?

- include details and examples to support each reason in the paragraphs?

- remember to indent the first line of each paragraph?

- remember to write neatly?

If you missed anything, go back now and add or change it!

The Conclusion

The last paragraph is the conclusion. This should be a brief summary of your essay. The conclusion should also begin with a transition word, followed by a comma, but this time it should begin with a conclusion transition word.

Some examples of conclusion transition words are:

in conclusion
in summary
to conclude
in brief
to sum up

After your transition word, restate your thesis. Then briefly sum up your three reasons. Finally, end your essay with one last sentence that wraps up everything. This last sentence can even be a call to action. A call to action is asking the reader to do something, like sign a petition, join a group, or write a letter. Since this is a summary of your essay, make sure that there is no new information in your conclusion.

Here is the conclusion for the uniform topic:

In conclusion, students should not be required to wear school uniforms. These uniforms could be uncomfortable and prevent students from listening to the lesson. Uniforms could also be too expensive for parents to afford. They can take away the individuality of the students. Let's let students be themselves!

Now, on the lines provided, write your conclusion for the extended school year topic.

_____

_____

_____

_____

_____

_____

_____

_____

Time to Check:

Did you:

- begin with the correct type of transition word?
- insert a comma after the transition?
- briefly restate your three reasons?
- remember to indent the first line of each paragraph?
- remember to write neatly?
- end the essay with a wrap-up sentence?
- add any new information? If so, make sure you take it out now!

Let's take a look now at the complete persuasive essay for the school uniform topic.

Imagine going to a school where everyone looks the same: the same clothes, the same colors, the same patterns. Sounds pretty boring, right? Well, that is something that might happen in our town if some people have their way. No one wants to be bored in school, whether it is by teachers or by what people wear. Therefore, students should not be required to wear school uniforms.

First, school uniforms can be very uncomfortable. They aren't made from the nicest fabrics and can be itchy and rough on skin. If students aren't comfortable in their clothes, they can become distracted and have trouble listening to the teacher and learning lessons. This could affect their grades in a negative way. Then students would be worried about their grades, and have another reason for not being able to concentrate in class.

Secondly, school uniforms may cost a lot of money. Parents may not be able to afford the cost of the uniform. If they can buy any type of clothes for their kids, then they can shop in places they can afford. They can even wait for the clothes to go on sale, or use store coupons. It isn't fair to force parents to pay more money than they have to for clothes.

Thirdly, students show their individuality through their clothes. Clothing is a way to express how you feel, or what interests you have, such as a sports team like the Yankees. Students need to have a way to express themselves. Clothing is one of those ways. Some people may get picked on by bullies for expressing themselves in a different way, but that isn't always true. The bullies will just find something else to make fun of about someone if everyone is dressed the same. Uniforms would take away one way to be an individual.

In conclusion, students should not be required to wear school uniforms. These uniforms could be uncomfortable and prevent students from listening to the lesson. Uniforms could also be too expensive for parents to afford. They can take away the individuality of the students. Let's let students be themselves!

MAKING SURE THE ESSAY IS GOOD ENOUGH

USING THE NJ REGISTERED HOLISTIC SCORING RUBRIC

We now have a completed essay, but how do we know it is good enough for the NJ ASK? Let's take a look at the essay according to the NJ Registered Holistic Scoring Rubric. This is the same rubric that will be used to score your own essay. A copy of the rubric can be found in the appendix of this book. It is best if you become familiar with this rubric. Your goal on the entire language arts test

is to receive at least a proficient score. A score of a 1, 2, or 3 marks you as having *partial command* of the essay part of the test, and may prevent you from getting a proficient score. A score of 4 or higher will help you to achieve a proficient score. You should review what is needed to score a 4 or higher on the essay. If you look at the 4 column, you will see what you need to include in order to score a 4.

You need to include:

- an opening and closing (introduction and conclusion)

- a single focus (you can't be for <u>and</u> against the issue)

- transitions

- some development of details

- readability (no one expects you to be perfect when it comes to grammar and punctuation, but you should not have so many errors that they prevent the reader from understanding what you are trying to say)

Take a look at the rest of the rubric. Some essays are nonscorable. This means they cannot be scored and therefore do not get any points. This does not often happen, but if the scorer reads the essay and finds that the writer has written too little or has written about the wrong topic, he or she will not be able to score the essay. Also, if a student does not write neatly, the evaluator may not be able to read it, and will not bother to score the essay. This will most likely cause the student to lose the chance to achieve a proficient score on the entire test.

Essays that receive scores of 1, 2, or 3 have many errors, are missing an opening, or closing, or sufficient details, and are not well organized. On the other hand, essays that receive a 5 or 6 take the essay a step further than those that receive a score of 4. These are the essays that include things like figurative language, have few or no errors, and have well-developed ideas that follow a logical flow or order. See the chart on the next page for a quick guide to what you need to do in order to receive a certain score. Keep this in mind when you are writing.

You don't have to be perfect in your first draft. You will have time to review if you listen to your teacher. He or she will let you know when you have about *ten minutes* left in the test. That is the time to go back, reread your essay, and decide how you can improve it.

Score	Requirements
1, 2, or 3	▪ many errors ▪ missing an opening or closing, or details ▪ not well organized
4	▪ an opening and closing (introduction and conclusion) ▪ a single focus (you can't be for <u>and</u> against the issue) ▪ transitions ▪ some development of details ▪ readability (no one expects you to be perfect when it comes to grammar and punctuation, but you should not have so many errors that they prevent the reader from understanding what you are trying to say)
5 or 6	▪ attempt compositional risks, like adding figurative language or complex sentences to the essay ▪ few or no errors ▪ well-developed ideas that follow a logical flow

WRITING WITH THE RUBRIC

With all of this in mind, let's take a look at the school uniform essay. Is the essay on topic? Does it follow the correct format, including an introduction, conclusion, and transitions? Does it have few errors, if any? The answer to all of these questions is YES. Therefore, the essay should be scored at least a 4 on the NJ Registered Holistic Scoring Rubric.

Let's now check to see if it can get a higher score. In order for it to receive a score of 5 on the rubric, the essay should have very few errors. Sure enough, it does. The essay also should have a single focus. It does have a single focus. There should be evidence of compositional risks. There aren't too many. The hook is pretty good; however, there is not much figurative language in the essay (for example, the use of similes). The essay also has a logical flow of ideas, but then again, there are not many details to support each of the three reasons. Taking all of this into consideration, this essay would probably be scored a 4.

Let's not just settle for a four! How could it be improved? Let's read it once again, only this time there have been improvements made to the essay. The improvements are in bold.

Imagine going to a school where everyone looks the same: the same clothes, the same colors, the same patterns. Sounds pretty boring, right? Well, that is something that might happen in our town if some people have their way. No one wants to be bored in school, whether it is by teachers or by what people wear. Therefore, students should not be required to wear school uniforms.

First, school uniforms can be very uncomfortable. They aren't made from the **finest** fabrics and can be itchy and rough on skin. If students aren't comfortable in their clothes, they can become distracted and have **difficulty** listening to the teacher and learning lessons. **Eventually this will negatively affect their grades. A student can be made to feel like a failure due to scratchy clothing.**

Secondly, school uniforms may cost a lot of money. Parents may not be able to afford the cost of the uniform. If they can buy any type of clothes for their **children** then they can shop in *clothing stores* they can afford. They can even wait for the clothes to go on sale, or use store coupons. It isn't fair to force parents to pay more money than they have to for clothes.

In addition, students show their individuality through their clothes. Clothing is a way to express how you feel, or what interests you have. For example, some students may be fans of a certain sports team, like the Yankees. They might like to show their support for the team by wearing clothing with the team's logo. This can help them to find a group where they fit in, and not feel so much like an outsider. Some people may get picked on by bullies for expressing themselves in a different way, but that isn't always true. The bullies will just find something else to make fun of about someone if everyone is dressed the same. *Adolescents* need to have a way to express themselves. Clothing is one of those ways. Uniforms would take away one way to be an individual.

In conclusion, students should not be required to wear school uniforms. These uniforms could be uncomfortable and prevent students from listening to the lesson. Uniforms could also be expensive. They can take away the individuality of the students. Let's let students be themselves **and encourage others to support this cause by speaking out in favor of choice in fashion for students!**

How has this essay been changed? First, some words have been changed to either improve vocabulary, or to be more specific. *Nicest* has been changed to *finest*, a stronger word, and *places* has been changed to a more specific word, *stores*. The adjective *clothing* was added so the reader knows exactly what the author is trying to say. Details were also added to the essay to expand a thought. One example is adding how students might feel if they cannot concentrate in class. This also adds a simile to the writing. The last statement also arranges for a **call to action**. The writer is asking the reader to speak out in favor of choice in fashion, and therefore to speak out against school uniforms. These improvements increase the writer's chances of getting a higher score for the essay.

USING THE RUBRIC TO EVALUATE AN ESSAY

Here is another essay to evaluate. First, read the essay and decide if it follows the correct guidelines for a persuasive essay. Then, use the NJ Registered Holistic Scoring Rubric to score it. Write your score and reasons below.

Writing Prompt: *Although after-school activities may be enjoyable for many students, schools must find the money to be able to fund and maintain these activities. Recently the school budget has been decreased. Due to this budget cut, the principal of your school has decided to eliminate all after-school activities in order to save money. Write a letter to the principal telling him or her what you think of the idea.*

I really don't think it's fair to cut the after-school activities. Why do we have to suffer just because people can't find enuf money for everything. Why can't we get the money from somewhere else. Many kids in school will be really upset about this desisin.

I belong to the robotics club after school. We have a lot of fun their Mr. Smith teaches us many fun things like how to build robots and make games. If we couldn't go to this club many of us would be bored at home.

Other students go to after school activities to. Their is cheerleading sports newspaper and Spanish clubs they all have lots of kids that would be upset if the clubs were canseld.

Maybe we could raise the money ourselfs. Their has to be a lot of ways to raise money. My sister is in the Girl Scouts and she sells cookies every year maybe we could do that it raises a lot of money for her club.

In concluson its not fair to cut our after school programs. I hope the principal understands that she is wrong. A lot of students would be upset. After school programs are good for kids so they are not bored at home. Thank you.

Write down what you would score this essay on the lines below and tell your reasons for your score.

_____

_____

_____

_____

_____

_____

_____

This essay would probably receive a score of 2. Did you notice that the writing prompt asked for the response to be in letter form? The essay is definitely not in letter form. The only hint of the writer directing this essay toward someone is the *thank you* at the end. If you are asked to write a response in letter form, you still should write the typical five-paragraph essay, but also include a greeting to the reader, a closing, and your signature. You don't need to include your first and last name—just your first name is fine, in order to maintain your privacy.

The writer also began the essay with the thesis, so there really is no proper introduction. There are many spelling and punctuation mistakes. For example, we see a pattern of mistakes using the incorrect spelling of the word *there*. The second two sentences in the essay begin with the word *why*. That should be a big signal that the sentences are asking a question, and should therefore end with a question mark. They do not. This essay also has run-on sentences that make it harder for the reader to understand what the author is trying to say. The author also uses the word *I* many times. This is a beginning of a persuasive essay; unfortunately, it needs a lot of editing. Don't make the same mistakes with your essay!

WRITING A COMPLETE ESSAY

PUTTING YOUR ESSAY TOGETHER

You have had practice writing parts of your own persuasive essay, as well as reading and evaluating two other pieces of writing. Here is your chance to put it all together. Remember what builds a strong, persuasive essay, and what can cause you to lose points from your final score. Take what you have written so far as separate sections for the extended school year prompt and put them all together in one complete persuasive essay. The Writer's Checklist on page 156 of this book can help you to remember your best writing style. It is the same checklist that will be given to you on the day of the test. You can use it as you write to help you remember to focus on your content, vocabulary, and mechanics, like spelling and grammar. When you are finished, check to see that you have included all the key parts of the essay, and that you have included them in the right order.

_____

_____

_____

_____

_____

_____

_____

_____

_____

_____

_____

_____

_____

_____

Time to Check:

Did you:

- ▪ include the correct information in the correct order in each paragraph?

- ▪ avoid using the phrase "I think" and bully words?

- ▪ use the Writer's Checklist to help you with your writing?

- ▪ remember to indent the first line of each paragraph?

- ▪ remember to write neatly?

TIME TO WRITE YOUR OWN!

Now you will have the chance to write a persuasive essay from start to finish. Read the new writing prompt, then brainstorm and write your essay. Remember what you have learned in this chapter! Then read the Time to Check section at the end to help you evaluate your essay. Try timing yourself so you can get used to writing a complete, revised persuasive essay in approximately 45 minutes. Keep in mind that you should brainstorm for 5–10 minutes and reserve the last 5–10 minutes for editing and revising your essay. That leaves you about 25–35 minutes to write your essay.

Writing Prompt: *Many students have been reporting that they are not satisfied with the choices offered for school lunch. The student council has proposed to the principal that the students have a voice in what is served for lunch. The proposal asks that one of the choices each day be selected by the student council, with input from the students. In order to allow for the new menu items, the price of student lunches will have to be increased. How do you feel about the proposal? Write a letter to the student council telling them what your thoughts are.*

Brainstorm here:

PROS	CONS

Begin your essay here:

_____

_____

_____

_____

_____

_____

_____

_____

_____

_____

_____

_____

_____

_____

Time to Check:

Did you:

- remember to reread the question and write down what it was asking?

- brainstorm?

- include the correct information in the correct order in each paragraph?

- avoid using the phrase "I think" and bully words?

- try to sound like a lawyer, writing your essay with the best words you know?

- use the Writer's Checklist to help you as you wrote your essay?

- remember to indent the first line of each paragraph?

- remember to write neatly?

- put your essay in letter format, if that is what it states to do in the prompt?

Look at the NJ Registered Holistic Scoring Rubric to evaluate your essay.

Think about what score you would probably be given and the reasons for the score. How did you do? Do you rate your essay with a 4 or higher? If so, great job! If not, check now to see how you can improve it. Don't worry, you'll get to practice writing another persuasive essay in the last chapter.

READING FOR MEANING

Another part of the Language Arts NJ ASK deals with reading stories and answering multiple-choice questions. You will be asked many types of questions after you read a short story. The story is also known as a passage. This can be easy for some students, but not so easy for others. Imagine this: You are given a passage to read. You come to the end only to realize you have no idea what you have just read because you were thinking about the party you are going to this weekend, or the football practice you have after school. Does this sound familiar? It happens to many students.

If this occurs in class, you can often reread the passage and go on from there. However, if you daydream during this part of the NJ ASK test, you may not have time to read the story again. Not only do you have to **focus on the story**, but you will also need to understand what the questions are asking.

By the time you finish this chapter, you will be prepared with tips to help you keep focused. You also will have practiced many of the types of questions you will see on the test.

This chapter contains warm-up passages, which concentrate on a certain concept, as well as sample passages, which contain many concepts learned in the chapter. The answers to all of the questions can be found in the appendix. You will see that the warm-up passage answers have an in-depth explanation in order to start you off on the right track.

In this chapter you will learn about:

- reading and understanding passages

- working with multiple-choice questions

- plot

- figurative language

- main idea, details, and purpose

- relationships in passages

READING AND UNDERSTANDING PASSAGES

The NJ ASK includes two sections where you will read several passages and answer questions after each passage. Most of the questions will be multiple-choice, concentrating on different concepts in the passage, and one or two will be open-ended. Skills for answering the open-ended questions will come in the next chapter. In this chapter, the focus is on reading the passage, understanding what you have just read, and then being able to understand and answer the multiple-choice questions that follow.

There will be two types of reading passages, fiction and non-fiction. As you may know, fiction stories are ones that aren't true. They can be fantasy stories that include talking animals or creatures from another planet. They can also be realistic stories that haven't actually happened. On the other hand, non-fiction passages are ones that are true. Often they are about a historical person or event. This chapter's passages are general reading passages, and they are there to help you get an idea of the types of questions that are on the NJ ASK. The passages on the actual test may be similar or may be from authentic literature. You will see some passages from authentic literature in the practice test chapter.

STAY FOCUSED

The first step for either type of writing is to understand the passage. Some students have trouble focusing on the material. They begin to daydream. This is a common problem, but one that students must try to overcome. As stated earlier, if you daydream while reading the passage, you may not have time during the test to reread the entire passage. This could cause a problem when it is time to answer the questions.

There are two strategies that can help you to keep your focus. First, read the questions *before* reading the passage. When you know the questions that you are about to have to answer, you can look for those answers in the passage as you are reading. If you have a goal as you are reading, this can help you to maintain your focus on the passage. However, make sure you read the entire passage *before* you answer the questions. This will make sure that you don't jump to conclusions about the answer before having all of the information.

A second strategy is to underline any information you think may be important in your booklet as you are reading. This serves two purposes. One is to help keep you focused. The other is to have ideas in the passage stand out so that you can find them easily when it comes time for you to answer the questions. Of course, if your teacher tells you not to underline in the booklet, then you shouldn't. The rules for the NJ ASK are constantly changing, and they may have changed since this book was written. Your teacher will have the most up-to-date information for you.

Here is a quick-reference chart of tips for reading passages:

Strategy	Tip
Strategy #1	Read the questions before reading the passage to help you keep focused on what you are reading. This will also help you find the information you need to answer the questions.
Strategy #2	Underline key words as you read the passage to help you locate important parts of the passage later. *NOTE: Only do this if your teacher says it is okay.

WORKING WITH MULTIPLE-CHOICE QUESTIONS

Multiple-choice questions can confuse some students. First, make sure you read the question carefully. Sometimes you can miss important parts of the question if you read it quickly. Words like *best* or *not* can change the meaning or the answer of a question. For example, read this question: *Which of the following is* not *a setting of the story?* Some students who don't read carefully might not see the word *not* in the sentence, look for an example of the setting, and then get the question wrong. Read the question, and then ask yourself if you really understand what the question is asking. Once you do know what it is asking, then you can fill in the answer.

CHOOSING THE BEST ANSWER

Sometimes you might understand what the question is asking but are not sure of the correct answer. Usually it is best to **go with your first instinct**, or gut feeling. If you read the question too many times, or second-guess yourself, you are liable to choose the wrong answer. You may be saying, "But what if I don't even have a gut feeling? Should I just take any guess?" The answer is no. This usually won't help. What you can do is try to eliminate as many of the possible answers as you can and then make an educated guess from the remaining answers. You can sometimes eliminate one or two answers that can't possibly be the correct answer for one reason or another. Then, at least you can **make an educated guess** from the other two choices either by going back to the passage, or by using your common sense. Here is an example.

What is a conjunction?

A. a chicken

B. your name

C. a word that connects two ideas

D. a pencil

Even if you don't know what a conjunction is, you should be able to eliminate answer B. You probably know that it isn't a pencil or chicken, either. Therefore the correct answer must be **C.** All questions might not be this easy, but you can use the strategy to help you find an answer. Just remember, if you have to go through this process, don't take too long. **The NJ ASK is a timed test.** If you are taking too long, you can skip the question and come back to it later, if you have time. Don't forget to make sure you move on to the correct number in your answer folder and test booklet!

Here is a quick-reference chart of tips for answering multiple-choice questions:

Tactic	Tip
Tactic #1	Read the question carefully and look for important words like *not* or *best*, which could change the meaning of the question. Make sure you understand what the question is asking.
Tactic #2	If you don't know the answer to a question, try to eliminate answers that don't make sense, or that you know can't be the answer.
Tactic #3	Remember that you are taking a timed test; don't spend too much time on any one test question.

PLOT

The plot is what actually happens in the story. If you took all of the events that take place in a story and put them together in order, they would create the plot. There are several parts of the plot:

- setting
- conflict
- characters
- climax
- resolution
- theme

The story is usually written from a certain point of view. The person or character telling the story determines the point of view, also known as the perspective. Two types that are commonly used: first person and third person. First person is where the narrator or main character tells the story to the reader. You can easily tell if a passage is written in first person because the words *I*, *me*, *us*, and *we* will be used very often. The character explains how he/she feels as the story is being told. Third person is when the author tells the story. The author will use words such as *he*, *she*, and *they*. The only time you will see the words *I*, *me*, *us*, and *we* is if a character is speaking, and the words will be in quotation marks.

SETTING

The setting of the story is not only where the story takes place, but also *when* the story occurs, like the time of day or time of year. The setting can affect the mood, or the feeling readers get as they read the story. If you watch or read a scary story, when and where does it take place? Usually this kind of story takes place somewhere dark and quiet. This setting gets the audience ready to be scared by the monster that's about to attack. This is exactly what the writer wants. If the setting were somewhere else, the audience might not be frightened. For example, the setting of a haunted house during a thunderstorm will give the reader a different feeling than the setting of a park on a sunny day.

CONFLICT

The conflict is the problem the main character(s) is/are faced with and must try to defeat. The conflict can be external, which means the problem is coming from somewhere around the character. This can be another character, some other creature, or even the environment. A conflict can also be internal. This is where the character has a problem deciding what to do. It is more of a mental problem for the character.

Example:

External	A prince must get through a dangerous blizzard to rescue the princess. The conflict is between the prince and the blizzard.
Internal	A character gets invited to a party, and wants to go, but the character's best friend is not invited. The character debates whether going to the party and possibly hurting the best friend's feelings is worth the fun of attending the party. In this case, the conflict is deciding whether or not to go to the party.

CHARACTERS

There are two types of main characters in a story. First, there is the protagonist. This is the character in the story that has a problem and needs to solve it. The other type is the antagonist. The antagonist is the character that creates the problem for the protagonist.

Here is an example of each from *"The Three Little Pigs,"* a story familiar to many:

Protagonist	The pigs are the protagonists because they face the problem of getting their houses blown down and must try to stop it from happening.
Antagonist	The antagonist is the wolf who is causing a problem for the pigs by trying to blow their houses down.

CLIMAX AND RESOLUTION

The climax of a story is where protagonists begin to have their problems solved. It is often the most exciting part of the story. The climax of *"The Three Little Pigs"* is when the wolf tries to blow down the brick house containing the pigs, but is unable to. The climax leads to the resolution. This is the part in the story where the protagonist's problem is solved, and it includes the other events that lead up to the ending. Once again, in *"The Three Little Pigs,"* the resolution is when the wolf runs off and leaves the pigs alone.

THEME

The theme of a story is the lesson we can learn from reading the story. From reading *"The Three Little Pigs,"* we learn that intelligence can sometimes be more important than strength. The last little pig is smart enough to build his house out of bricks. The wolf's strong exhale is no match for the bricks, and the wolf is defeated. Stories can sometimes have more than one theme.

Often writers use sensory language to give the reader a better idea of what is happening in the story. Sensory language includes any type of details that relate to the senses, what the characters see, hear, touch, taste, or smell. Writers also use symbols in their writing. Symbols are objects that represent an idea like love, anger, or fear. For example, the wolf in *"The Three Little Pigs"* can symbolize wickedness.

> Note: If you are afraid that you won't remember all of these concepts, don't worry. There is a Quick-reference List on page 65, just before the sample passages. It lists all the terms and their definitions, along with examples.

Read the following passage and answer the questions about its plot. Remember, the answers can be found in the appendix of this book.

The Notebook

"Someone stole my notebook!" I yelled out in the middle of class. My comment startled not only the other students but our teacher, Mr. Klein, as well. I didn't mean for it to come out that way, but when I realized my notebook was missing, the words just rushed out of my 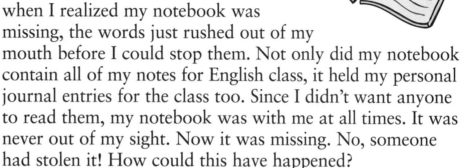 mouth before I could stop them. Not only did my notebook contain all of my notes for English class, it held my personal journal entries for the class too. Since I didn't want anyone to read them, my notebook was with me at all times. It was never out of my sight. Now it was missing. No, someone had stolen it! How could this have happened?

I was snapped back to reality by Mr. Klein's stern comment, "Was yelling out really necessary, Ms. Martinez?" He always referred to us by our last names when he was upset with something we had done. I knew I was in trouble, but I had a really good reason for my behavior. Mr. Klein had to know that my outburst was simply reaction to the dreadful event that had occurred.

As I was pleading my case to Mr. Klein, I had an insight into what must have happened, and it hit me like a ton of bricks. It had to be Josephine! Yes, Josephine took—no, *stole*—my journal. She'd been dying to get her grubby little hands on it ever since she heard that I wrote something bad about her in it. She confronted me about this about a week ago. I tried to explain to her that I never wrote about her in the journal. The truth is I had plenty of better things to write about. Josephine was not listening and kept saying that she would find out the truth, no matter what. She was the one who took my journal, and now there was no telling what she would do with it.

After English class, and on the way to lunch, I explained what had happened to my friends. I didn't know how I was going to do it, but I was going to confront Josephine and make her give me back my notebook. I needed a plan. I pulled all of us into the girl's room for some privacy.

"Do you have any ideas?" I asked my friends. It was the first time all of us were silent. Everyone just shrugged their shoulders and shook their heads. Obviously I was going to have to be the mastermind and create the plan myself.

Suddenly it was like a lightbulb turned on in my brain. I turned to the others and shouted, "I've got it!" The girls all stared at me, concentrating on every word I said. "Rosa, you will go over to Josephine when she is at her locker and ask her for notebook paper. She will have to go through her locker to pull out her notebook to get the paper. While she is doing that, Janeece, you peek in her locker to check to see if my notebook is in there. You know what my notebook looks like, right?"

"Sure, it's pink with white dots on it," she replied.

"Great," I added. "I will be waiting around the corner. When you see my notebook, nod your head. When you give me that sign, I will run over and grab it from her locker. I will catch her red-handed!"

We walked out of the bathroom and into the hallway lined with rows of lockers. Just then we saw Josephine walking toward hers. I ducked around the corner. The plan went into action. It all happened so fast. Before I knew it, I saw Janeece nod her head. I ran out and yelled, "Gotcha!" I then grabbed the pink notebook sticking out of Josephine's locker.

Josephine replied, "What are you doing?"

"You stole my notebook, and I'm taking it back," I answered.

Just then I looked down at the notebook and realized it wasn't mine. It was pink, but it had yellow dots on it. Janeece must have seen only that it was pink and thought it was mine. I didn't know what to say. All of a sudden I heard my name being yelled from down the hall. It was my friend Patty.

"Hi Maria!" Patty said excitedly. "I have been looking for you everywhere. You dropped this in the hall this morning."

She handed me my pink notebook with white dots. I was so happy to have it, but then I realized what I had done to Josephine. After that Josephine gave me an annoyed look, shook her head, and walked away. It was then I knew I had some apologizing to do.

I said to my friends, "Can you help me come up with a new plan to apologize to Josephine?" They all groaned and walked away. Some people just don't like planning, I guess.

Warm-up Drill #1

1. What is the *first* setting of the story?

   A. the girl's room

   B. the classroom

   C. the cafeteria

   D. the hallway

2. What kind of person is Maria?

   A. mean

   B. quiet

   C. strong-minded

   D. insecure

3. Which statement best describes the conflict of the story?

   A. The main character has a fight with another character in the story.

   B. The main character must develop a plan to get her missing notebook back.

   C. The main character's friends do not want to help her find her notebook.

   D. The main character is missing her notebook, which is filled with important information.

4. The protagonist in the story is:

   A. Maria.

   B. Janeece.

   C. Patty.

   D. Josephine.

5. Which of the following is part of the story's climax?

   A. Maria yells out in the middle of class.

   B. Maria snatches the notebook from Josephine's locker.

   C. Josephine walks away from Maria.

   D. Maria wants to come up with a plan to apologize to Josephine.

6. Which *best* describes the general plot of this story?

   A. Maria realizes her notebook is missing, blames Josephine for stealing it, comes up with a plan to get her notebook back, then finds out that she accidentally dropped it in the hallway and feels bad for accusing Josephine of stealing her book.

   B. Maria realizes her notebook is missing, Josephine accuses Maria of writing about her in her notebook, Patty tells Maria that Maria dropped her notebook in the hallway, and they all become friends.

   C. Josephine accuses Maria of writing about her in her notebook, Maria accuses Josephine of stealing her notebook, Maria comes up with a plan to get her notebook back, and they all become friends.

   D. Josephine accuses Maria of writing about her in her notebook, Maria yells back at Josephine, Maria loses her notebook and blames Josephine for stealing it, and Maria feels bad for accusing Josephine of stealing her book.

7. How is the conflict resolved?

   A. Maria apologizes to Josephine.

   B. Josephine admits stealing the notebook.

   C. Maria finds the notebook hidden in Josephine's locker.

   D. Patty tells Maria she found her notebook and hands it back to her.

8. Which of the following could be this story's theme?

    A. Keep your notebook close to you.

    B. Making plans is fun.

    C. It is not good to assume. —

    D. Teachers like it when students yell in class.

9. The author uses Maria's notebook to symbolize:

    A. friendship.

    B. cruelty.

    C. happiness.

    D. identity. —

10. The story is written from which perspective?

    A. first person —

    B. third person

    C. second person

    D. none of the above

Answers are on pages 147–149.

FIGURATIVE LANGUAGE

Figurative language is used by writers to help the reader picture what is going on in the story. This type of writing cannot be taken literally. In other words, the words have a different meaning from what they actually say. For example: *Her face was as red as a cherry.* Does this mean that the girl's skin actually turned red? No, instead it has another meaning. We might say that someone's face turns red because they are blushing and their cheeks get a bit redder than usual. This could be because the person is angry or embarrassed. Here is another example: *The old house seemed to say, "Stay out!"* This doesn't mean that the house really spoke.

The sentence has another meaning. Can you take a guess as to what it really means? The sentence means that the way the house looked from the outside gave us the feeling that it was old, abandoned, and did not want visitors.

There are several types of figurative language. This type of writing will most likely show up on the NJ ASK. In order to make sure that you are familiar with it, here are the most common types of figurative language:

■ Simile—A simile is a comparison of two different things. When comparing these two things, the word like or as is used. For example: *He was as tall as the Empire State Building*. This is a simile comparing a man and a building. The comparison uses the word *as*. This is definitely a simile, but what does it mean? It means that the man is very tall. When we think of the Empire State Building, we think of a very tall building. Therefore, the man must be very tall if we are comparing him to the Empire State Building.

■ Metaphor—A metaphor, like a simile, compares two things. However it has one major difference. A metaphor does not use the word *like* or *as*. *The man was the Empire State Building standing over us* is an example of a metaphor. This also makes a comparison between the man and the Empire State Building, but did you notice that the metaphor does not use the word *like* or *as*? Instead, it states that the man was the building. This comparison also tells the reader that the man is tall, but it is a metaphor instead of a simile.

■ Personification—Personification gives a non-human character human traits. Here's an example: *The lock on the fence told us to keep out*. Does the writer literally mean that the lock spoke? If not, what does this statement mean? The lock does not actually speak, but the characters in the story know that the lock on the gate means that they should not open it. This is an example of personification because the lock isn't human, but the writer has given it a human trait, speaking.

■ Hyperbole—A hyperbole is an extreme exaggeration the writer uses to create an effect in the story. *I had about one million pages to read for homework last night* is a hyperbole. It doesn't mean that the character literally had one million pages to read. Instead, the writer wants the reader to understand that the character is complaining about doing the homework and exaggerating to prove that there was a lot to do.

Now that you have learned the types of figurative language, read the following passage and answer the questions that follow. Remember, the answers can be found in the appendix of this book.

Baby-sitting

"Make sure Matty doesn't get into trouble while I'm gone," Jamie's mother said.

"I know, I know. I've done this a million times before," Jamie answered.

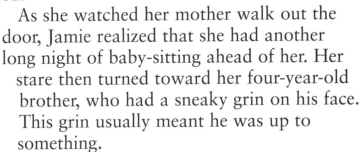

As she watched her mother walk out the door, Jamie realized that she had another long night of baby-sitting ahead of her. Her stare then turned toward her four-year-old brother, who had a sneaky grin on his face. This grin usually meant he was up to something.

Just then, her brother darted up the stairs as fast as a cheetah. Jamie ran after him. She had trouble keeping up. He was lightning racing across the top floor of the house. By the time she caught up to him, she noticed he had something in his hand. It was a small piece of construction paper with a red heart on it. He handed the heart to Jamie. Even though there was no writing on it, she knew that the card said that her brother loved her. She could tell by the smile on his chubby little face. Jamie then realized that the night might not be so bad. But she was still glad Matty wasn't twins!

Warm-up Drill #2

1. Which statement from the passage is an example of personification?

   A. She was glad Matty wasn't twins.

   B. She watched her mother walk out the door.

   C. She knew that the card said he loved her.

   D. She could tell by the smile on his chubby little face.

2. The part of the passage that says, *"He was lightning racing across the top floor,"* is an example of:

   A. personification.

   B. a metaphor.

   C. a simile.

   D. a hyperbole.

3. The purpose of using the simile *"like a cheetah"* is to:

   A. tell how Matty climbs up the stairs.

   B. describe how quickly Matty moves.

   C. show why Matty left the room.

   D. show what kind of character Matty is.

4. Which statement from the passage is an example of a hyperbole?

   A. I've done this a million times before.

   B. She then realized that the night might not be so bad.

   C. She was still glad Matty wasn't twins!

   D. Jamie realized that she had another long night of baby-sitting ahead of her.

5. This story is written from which point of view?

   A. first person

   B. second person

   C. third person —

   D. none of the above

Answers are on pages 149–150.

MAIN IDEA, DETAILS, AND PURPOSE

Non-fiction passages have a central thought that they are trying to explain to the reader. This central thought is called the main idea. The main idea is what the paragraph or passage is mostly about. It usually can be found at the beginning of the paragraph, but it is not always found there. In order to have a full paragraph, the writer needs to add more information about the main idea. This information is called details. Details tell more about the main idea and give you more of an understanding of what you are reading.

The author of the passage often has a purpose for writing about a topic. The purpose may be to tell you how the author feels about a topic, or even to persuade you to feel a certain way about a subject. To persuade means to try to get the reader to think the way the author thinks. The author usually doesn't state his or her feelings openly. Instead, the reader gets a sense of how the author feels by certain things that are said in the paragraph. For example, consider the following sentence: *The marvelous creature stood on top of the hill looking down at its prey.* How do you think the author feels about the creature in the sentence? Chances are the author likes the creature because, even though the creature is about to attack its prey, the author still calls it marvelous, another word for *wonderful*. The author doesn't have to say that he or she likes the creature. Readers know this by the way the writer describes the creature, calling it marvelous.

VOCABULARY IN CONTEXT

Vocabulary is important in all types of writing. Have you ever read a book or passage and come to a word that you don't know? What do you do? Your first instinct may be to skip it, but then you may lose the meaning of the paragraph. Instead, you may decide to look it up in a dictionary, ask a friend what it means, or ask your teacher to help you. On the NJ ASK, however, you cannot do any of these things. Does that mean that you should just skip over the word and hope for the best? That may not be the best idea for two reasons. First, you may lose the meaning of the paragraph. Second, there may be a multiple-choice question that asks you to define this word. Not to worry—there are context clues to help you.

Context clues are words or sentences near the word you don't know that can help you to understand what the confusing word means. For example: *The pie was so delectable that I couldn't wait for a second helping.* You may not know what the word *delectable* means, but if you read the sentence carefully, you can figure it out. The pie was delectable, and a pie is something you usually eat. If you want some more of something, it must mean that it tastes good, so therefore delectable must mean that something tastes good. Using context clues can mean the difference between understanding a paragraph and being stuck on a word.

Read the following passage and answer the questions about the main idea, details, and author's purpose. Remember, the answers can be found in the appendix of this book.

Trenton

New Jersey's capital, Trenton has an interesting history. It was first established by the Quakers in 1679. By 1719, the town took on the name "Trent-towne." It was named after one of the major landholders of the time, William Trent. Eventually "Trent-towne" became Trenton. Trenton was the site of George Washington's first military victory during the time of the Revolutionary War. Washington won many other battles. For a period of time, Trenton was so significant that it was chosen as the capital of the United States. Later, in 1790, it became the capital of New Jersey, and it has been the capital ever since.

Warm-up Drill #3

1. What is the main idea of the paragraph?

   A. Trenton was originally called "Trent-towne."

   B. In 1790, Trenton became the capital of New Jersey

   C. New Jersey's capital has an interesting history. —

   D. Trenton was named after William Trent.

2. What does the word *significant* mean in the paragraph?

   A. important —

   B. violent

   C. minor

   D. big

3. Based on this passage, how does the author feel about Trenton?

    A. The author wants us to stop talking about it.

    B. The author thinks the city is important.

    C. The author thinks it was only important to the Quakers.

    D. The author thinks Trenton is only important to George Washington.

4. Which detail does *not* belong in the paragraph?

    A. By 1719, the town took on the name "Trent-towne."

    B. Washington won many other battles.

    C. It was named after one of the major landholders of the time, William Trent.

    D. It was first established by the Quakers in 1679.

Answers are on page 150.

RELATIONSHIPS IN PASSAGES

The NJ ASK will also include multiple-choice questions that ask you about the relationships in a passage. These relationships are compare-contrast, cause-effect, and inference. Comparing is telling how two ideas are alike. Contrasting is telling how those same two ideas are different. For instance, **compare and contrast** the wolf in *"Little Red Riding Hood"* and the wolf in *"The Three Little Pigs."* One example of a comparison is that both wolves are alike because they try to eat innocent characters in the story. However, they are different because one wolf does not try to hide himself, while the other disguises himself as Little Red's grandmother. You may be able to come up with many examples, but the important thing is to think about the relationship based on what the question is asking.

Cause and effect relationships are those that depend on one another. The cause not only comes before the effect but also makes it happen. The effect is the result. Think about taking a test. If someone does not study for a test, what is probably going to happen? The student will probably not do well, right? Well, the cause is not studying and the effect is not doing well on the test. Not studying can *cause* you to not do well on a test.

Inferring requires you to draw a conclusion about something in a passage based on the information that the author has provided. Basically you, the reader, have to make an educated guess about something in the passage. Read this example: *Gina and Rosita are best friends and in the same class. If Rosita is in sixth grade, what can we infer about Gina?* We are told that the girls are in the same grade. We also know that Rosita is in sixth grade. Based on these two facts, we can infer that Gina is in the sixth grade also. We are not told this specifically, but we can make a pretty good guess based on what we know.

An additional skill you will be required to demonstrate is being able to tell fact from opinion. A **fact** is something that is true and can be proven. An **opinion** is what someone believes about a topic. A fact is that George Washington was the first president of the United States. We can look up this information to prove it in a history textbook or an encyclopedia. An opinion is that George Washington was the best president. There is no absolute proof of this, and other people may say that another president was the best. Be careful because authors often try to make their opinions sound like facts, especially when they are trying to persuade you to agree with them.

Read the following passage and answer the questions about comparing, contrasting, inferring, facts, opinions, and cause and effect relationships. Remember, the answers can be found in the appendix of this book.

A Home for the Mets

The New York Mets will be playing in a new stadium in the spring of 2009. This new ballpark will be called Citi Field. For decades, Shea Stadium has been the Mets' home. There will be no need to travel any further to get to a game; Citi Field will be located next to Shea Stadium in Flushing, New York.

Mets followers will see some familiar things in the new stadium. It will still include concession stands that offer hot dogs and cheeseburgers to hungry fans, a picnic area, and natural grass on the field. This stadium will also hold over 40,000 people, just like Shea, rooting for the home team.

Fans that go to buy something to eat will not have to worry about missing the game anymore. The new stadium will have an open view of the field from all concession stands. In addition, when people get back to their seats, they will now be able to enjoy the increased leg room between all of the rows in the ballpark. The spring of 2009 will bring fans applauding not only the Mets, but the stadium as well.

Warm-up Drill #4

1. We can *infer* from the passage that:

   A. people will enjoy increased leg room in the new stadium.

   B. twice the number of people will now go to Mets games.

   C. after the spring of 2009, the Mets will no longer play in Shea Stadium.

   D. fans will have to travel farther to get to a Mets game.

2. What is an effect of the open view from the concession stands?

   A. Fans will not have to miss seeing the game. ⌐

   B. Fans will enjoy more leg room.

   C. Fans will eat in the picnic area.

   D. Fans will park near Shea Stadium.

3. The purpose of the second paragraph in the passage is to:

   A. compare Citi Field and Shea Stadium. ⌐

   B. contrast Citi Field and Shea Stadium.

   C. list the facts about the food served at the ballpark.

   D. describe the grass on the field.

4. Which of the following is an opinion?

   A. When people get back to their seats, they will now be able to enjoy the increased leg room between all of the rows in the ballpark.

   B. The New York Mets will be playing in a new stadium in the spring of 2009.

   C. This stadium will hold over 40,000 people, just like Shea, rooting for the home team.

   D. The spring of 2009 will bring fans applauding not only the Mets, but the stadium as well. ⌐

Answers are on page 151.

A QUICK-REFERENCE LIST OF KEY TERMS

1. Main Idea—the central idea that the passage or paragraph is talking about.

2. Details—ideas that tell more about the main idea.

3. Author's Purpose/Point of View—the reason why the author is writing his/her story or how the author feels about the topic in the story.

4. Figurative Language—a way of writing that doesn't mean exactly what it says. Instead it has a different meaning than what is written. There are many types:

   ▪ Simile—comparing two unlike things using the word *like* or *as*. Example: Her face was as red as a cherry.

   ▪ Metaphor—comparing two unlike things *without* using *like* or *as*. Example: He was the Empire State Building standing over us.

   ▪ Personification—giving human characteristics to non-human characters. Example: The frog smiled at the girl.

   ▪ Hyperbole—an extreme exaggeration. Example: I had a million pages to read last night.

   ▪ Sensory Details/Imagery—details that relate to the senses: what characters can see, hear, smell, taste, or touch in the story.

5. Plot—The events that happen in a story, or what the story is about. There are many parts of the plot:

   ▪ Setting—where the story takes place and the time it takes place. Example: One setting in *"Little Red Riding Hood"* is Grandma's house.

   ▪ Conflict—a problem between two characters in the story or a character and the environment. Example: A conflict in *"Little Red Riding Hood"* is between

Little Red Riding Hood and the wolf who is trying to eat her.

■ Theme—the "big idea" in a story or what we can learn from the story. Example: One of the themes in *"Little Red Riding Hood"* could be to listen to your parents. Little Red didn't listen to her mother by straying from the path to Grandma's house, thereby causing her to be in danger.

■ Resolution—how the conflict is solved. Example: The conflict is solved in *"Little Red Riding Hood"* when the woodsman saves Little Red Riding Hood by killing the wolf.

■ Climax—This is the most exciting part of the story. It is usually where the main character begins to solve the conflict. Example: The climax in *"Little Red Riding Hood"* is when the woodsman comes in.

■ Mood—the feeling you get from the writer's words in a story. Example: The mood in a story about a haunted house would be different from the mood in a story about going to a birthday party.

6. Cause and Effect—The cause comes first, and then it makes something else happen. Example: The girl left her toys in the middle of the floor. The mother tripped and fell over the toys. The cause is leaving the toys in the middle of the floor, and the effect is that the mother tripped.

7. Making Inferences—This is when you can assume or guess something in a story that isn't told to you directly. This is not just *any* guess; it is a guess based on other facts in the story. Example: He is sitting on the brown chair. The brown chair is in the kitchen. We can then *infer* that he is sitting in the kitchen. We haven't been told this directly, but based on the other facts, we can assume this.

8. Compare and Contrast—When you are asked to compare and contrast two characters or things in a story, you should tell how they are alike and different. Comparing is telling how they are alike. Contrasting is telling how they are different.

9. Point of View—the perspective the author uses to write. There are two main types:

   ▪ First Person—The writer tells the story from his or her point of view, or the main character's point of view. You will see the author use many *I*'s and *we*'s in the story. The story is being told directly to you, the reader.

   ▪ Third Person—This is when the author tells about the characters and what they do in the story. You won't see the words *I* or *me* used much, unless it is a quote from a character.

SAMPLE PASSAGES

Read each passage and answer the questions that follow. Remember to check your answers with the correct answers in the appendix of this book.

The Rainout

"This isn't fair, mom!" I protested.

"This isn't about fairness, Billy. You know you're still grounded," my mother replied.

I was the only one out of my group of friends who wasn't allowed to go to the Yankees game. This infuriated me so much that I stomped up the stairs and slammed my bedroom door shut. So what if I was still being punished for the low grade I received in math on my report card! Everyone was going, and

I *was* working harder. I had actually been doing my homework and studying. After all, my last test grade in the class was a B. Couldn't my mother see that I was trying? Either she couldn't see that, or maybe if she did, she didn't care. I'd tried to tell her that I'd learned my lesson, but she never, ever listens to me. I felt like a caged bird. I was only allowed out of the house to go to school, and then had to come straight home.

The clock reached 5:30, the time my friends were all meeting at Mark's house in order to carpool to the stadium. Each minute that passed by made my teeth clench tighter and tighter. How could this be happening to me?

Then, all of a sudden, through the open window in my room, I felt a strong breeze. A moment later I got a whiff of a familiar odor, the scent of the first few raindrops at the beginning of a rainstorm. I dashed to the window just in time to see the downpour. Then, a lightning bolt streaked across the sky. It was followed by a loud "boom!" I was so startled that I jumped up and bumped my head on the window sill. At that point reality hit me. The game would probably be rained out! I wasn't going to miss it! There would also probably be a make-up game. That game might take place after my grounding was over. As I thought about it, my jaw relaxed and even began to form a smile. I figured I should go and review my math homework, just to make sure I was ready for the next game!

Warm-up Drill #5

1. The phrase in the passage *"like a caged bird"* is an example of:

   A. a metaphor.

   B. a simile.

   C. personification.

   D. imagery.

2. We can *infer* that the loud *"boom!"* in the story is caused by:

   A. a tree that fell.

   B. the window slamming.

   C. the rain.

   D. thunder.

3. In the third paragraph, what does the word *infuriated* mean?

   A. angered

   B. excited

   C. saddened

   D. upset

4. This passage is written from which perspective?

   A. first person

   B. second person

   C. third person

   D. fourth person

5. Which of the following is a conflict in the story?

   A. Billy does not like when it rains.

   B. Billy's mother is mean.

   C. Billy cannot go to the game because of his poor grade.

   D. Billy cannot play baseball.

6. The sentence, *"I'd tried to tell her that I'd learned my lesson, but she never, ever listens to me,"* is an example of:

   A. a hyperbole.

   B. personification.

   C. a metaphor.

   D. a simile.

7. What is an effect of the rainstorm?

   A. Billy becomes angry.

   B. Billy begins to smile.

   C. Billy's friends do not go to the game.

   D. Billy is no longer grounded.

8. Which of the following describes the plot of the story?

   A. The main character is upset about being grounded, complains to his mother about not being able to go to a baseball game, and then she decides to let him go.

   B. The main character is upset about being grounded, complains to his mother about not being able to go to a baseball game, and then a storm gives him another chance to go to the game.

   C. The main character is upset about being grounded and not able to go to a baseball game, storms up to his room, and watches the game on television.

   D. The main character wants to go to a baseball game with his friends, but it is rained out and he is disappointed.

9. The theme of this story can best be stated as:

   A. People must accept the consequences of their actions.

   B. You can get your way if you yell enough.

   C. Rain storms make you feel better.

   D. Parents are unfair.

10. In the passage, the author uses the rain to symbolize:

   A. unfairness.

   B. anger.

   C. baseball.

   D. opportunity.

Answers are on page 152.

Famous "New Jerseyans"

Many people who have made an impact on the world have come from New Jersey. This tiny state has produced some big names in the world of politics, literature, history, sports, science, and music. Some of these famous figures have been vital to the development of the United States. Others have provided enjoyment for many fans all over the world.

When it comes to studying history, lots of people would recognize names like Aaron Burr, Grover Cleveland, and Molly Pitcher. Aaron Burr was born in Newark, New Jersey, and is known for challenging Alexander Hamilton to a duel. Prior to this challenge, Burr was vice-president of the United States. Grover Cleveland, born in Caldwell, New Jersey, was the twenty-fourth president of the United States. Molly Ludwig, also known as Molly Pitcher, was born near Trenton, New Jersey. She carried pitchers of water to her husband and other soldiers during the Revolutionary War.

The United States Space Program would not be complete without two astronauts who were born in New Jersey. Edwin "Buzz" Aldrin was born in Montclair in 1930. He became the second man, after Neil Armstrong, to walk on the moon. Walter Schirra was born in Englewood in 1923. He traveled aboard Mercury 7 and was also a member of the Gemini and Apollo programs.

In the world of music, many people are fans of the music of Frank Sinatra, Bruce Springsteen, Jon Bon Jovi, and Queen Latifah. These proud "New Jerseyans" have made their mark in the music industry, selling millions of records. Coming from the southern part of the state are Jon Bon Jovi and Bruce Springsteen. Bruce Springsteen's band is named the E Street Band. Queen Latifah, rapper, singer, and actress, was raised in the city of Newark. Frank Sinatra, one of the greatest singers of all time, was born in Hoboken.

All Yankee fans, and most baseball fans, would recognize the name Derek Jeter. He is an esteemed shortstop and team captain. Jeter was born in Pequannock. Shaquille O'Neal, basketball star and actor, was born in Newark, the same city as Queen Latifah. Judy Blume is also well-known, but not for being an athlete. She is a famous author of children's books. Judy Blume was born in Elizabeth, New Jersey.

New Jersey has produced many people whose contributions have impacted the United States, and even the world. They have played a role in various aspects of society. Even though these well known "New Jerseyans" come from different backgrounds, they have one thing in common. They have called New Jersey "home."

Warm-up Drill #6

1. Which is the main idea of paragraph three?

   A. Edwin "Buzz" Aldrin was born in Montclair in 1930.

   B. Walter Schirra was born in Englewood in 1923.

   C. The United States Space Program would not be complete without two astronauts who were born in New Jersey.

   D. Buzz Aldrin was important to the United States Space Program.

2. We can *infer* from the passage that Molly Pitcher:

   A. was a soldier in the Revolutionary War.

   B. got her nickname from carrying pitchers of water to soldiers.

   C. was a very intelligent woman.

   D. helped to win the war.

3. Which detail does *not* belong in the passage?

   A. Bruce Springsteen's band is named the E Street Band.

   B. Judy Blume is also well known, but not for being an athlete.

   C. Molly Ludwig, also known as Molly Pitcher, was born near Trenton, New Jersey.

   D. This tiny state has produced some big names in the world of politics, literature, history, sports, science, and music.

4. What does the word *vital* mean in the first paragraph?

   A. important

   B. minor

   C. harmful

   D. enjoyable

5. Which of the following is an opinion?

   A. Judy Blume is also well known, but not for being an athlete.

   B. He traveled aboard Mercury 7 and was also a member of the Gemini and Apollo programs.

   C. Grover Cleveland, born in Caldwell, New Jersey, was the twenty-fourth president of the United States.

   D. Frank Sinatra, one of the greatest singers of all time, was born in Hoboken.

6. The purpose of paragraph three is to:

   A. tell the types of space programs.

   B. tell the contributions of two astronauts from New Jersey.

   C. explain how important space travel is.

   D. explain the types of space travel.

7. In the fifth paragraph, the word *esteemed* most nearly means:

   A. average.

   B. self-confidence.

   C. admired.

   D. unimportant.

8. What is the main idea of the passage?

   A. Many famous people have come from New Jersey.

   B. Many athletes have been born in New Jersey.

   C. Bruce Springsteen, Jon Bon Jovi, and Frank Sinatra are famous singers.

   D. Buzz Aldrin was the second man to walk on the moon.

Answers are on page 153.

Chapter 4

ANSWERING OPEN-ENDED QUESTIONS

You already know how to read for meaning. However, there is more to the reading passage section than just reading a passage and then answering multiple-choice questions. There will also be two open-ended questions for you to answer in each section. Answering this type of question involves not only responding to what is being asked, but also providing examples from the passage and your own experiences.

In this chapter you will:

■ learn how to set up your answer and understand how you will be scored

■ learn how to use the ANSWER strategy to check your work

■ read sample passages and open-ended questions

SETTING UP YOUR ANSWER AND HOW YOU WILL BE SCORED

After answering the multiple-choice questions that go along with the reading passage, you will see two open-ended questions. The open-ended questions are to be answered on the lines provided on a separate page in your answer booklet. Just as with answering multiple-choice questions, first read the question carefully to make sure that you know what it is asking. Most of the time, the question will ask you for your opinion about something that happens in the passage. Once you are sure that you understand the question, make sure that you make a mental note of how many parts the question has for you to answer. Make sure that you restate the question as part of your answer. Also, don't forget to respond to each part so that you receive the maximum number of points possible.

In answering the question, it is always a good idea to use your best writing skills. That means making sure you use complete sentences, proper grammar, punctuation, spelling, and writing as neatly as you can. Remember, the evaluators do not know you, so they will not try to figure out what you are saying if your handwriting is too sloppy or your answer doesn't make sense. He or she will just give you a low score. Also, this is a time to use your top vocabulary, but just as in writing the persuasive essay, use vocabulary words that you know make sense in the response.

It is a good idea to become familiar with the rubric that will be used to score the open-ended questions. The rubric can be found in the appendix of this book. This rubric is different from the one that is used to score the persuasive essay or picture prompt. It ranges from 0 to 4. The highest score you can get is a 4. Based on this rubric, in order to get the highest score, first you need to answer all parts of the question correctly. In addition, the answers must show a deep understanding of the material and provide an explanation or opinion about the topic based on information in the text. Students need to include examples from the passage and/or their own life in order to score a four. Remember, the question will usually ask for your opinion, so include it, but also include the information to prove that you are right. That information comes from the passage and your experiences. A score of 3 would be given if a student answers the question correctly, but only provides a partial example or explanation in the answer.

A student would receive a score of 2 if the answer is not entirely correct or the examples are not totally appropriate. A score of 1 would be given if the answer is incomplete or does not provide good examples from the text. A response that receives a 0 does not answer the question.

THE ANSWER STRATEGY

In order to make sure that an open-ended question is answered correctly, you can use the *ANSWER* strategy. By using the *ANSWER* Strategy, you will be able to answer an open-ended question properly. Each letter in the word *answer* will help you to complete a task and get you one step closer to receiving a high score. The strategy is listed in the table. It is a good idea to try to memorize this strategy so that it can help you to provide a complete answer.

A	Always read the question carefully. ■ Do you understand what the question is asking? If not, read it again.
N	Notice how many parts there are to answer.
S	Start each sentence with an appropriate word and not a *conjunction*. ■ Examples of conjunctions are **and, but, or, because.**
W	Write neatly and make sure you use complete sentences and correct punctuation.
E	Examples from the text and your own life should be included in your answer.
R	Review your answer. ■ Did you answer what the question was asking? ■ Did you restate the question in your answer? ■ Did you answer each part of the question? ■ Did you include examples?

Note: You may come to an open-ended question that asks you to list information. Make sure you include this information in paragraph form, and not just a bulleted list.

SAMPLE PASSAGES AND OPEN-ENDED QUESTIONS

Now that you know how to answer an open-ended question, here is your chance to use that knowledge. Read the following passage and the open-ended question that follows. Then read the sample answer.

The Price of Being Popular

"Brrrrring!" The ring of the telephone woke me out of my trance. I picked up the cordless phone and saw on the caller ID that it was my friend June.

"Hi," I said after pressing the talk button.

"So what are you going to do?" replied June.

"About what?" I asked.

"You know what," answered June with an angered tone.

"Oh, you mean about Jessica," I replied.

"Yes, that's what I mean."

"I'm not sure. I have to think about it some more."

"Okay, just remember the party is important."

"I will. I'll call you back later."

I knew exactly what June meant from the beginning, but I was hoping she wouldn't bring up the subject. Jessica had been a friend of both of us since the first grade. The three of us were very close, but Jessica and I were inseparable. We did everything together: sleepovers, camp, birthday parties. We had great fun. That was until this year. We got to middle school and everything seemed to change. June and I were in most of the same classes, but Jessica wasn't. We were making new friends, but all Jessica cared about was hanging out with us. I tried to combine everyone, my new friends and old, but it didn't seem to work. My new friends didn't seem to like Jessica. They said she was boring and too quiet. I knew Jessica was quiet, but she was a really great person, and once she got to know you, Jessica could really be funny. However, my new friends didn't want to get to know her.

I did a great job of keeping the two groups separate. I'd hang out with Jessica and June one time, and then hang out with my new friends and June another. If Jessica asked me what I was doing that night, I would just tell her that I was staying home with my family. It was a perfect plan until last week. Jessica asked us to come over to eat pizza and watch a movie next Friday. June said she couldn't go. She had a wedding to go to that night. I told Jessica it was a great idea. I even offered to bring the popcorn.

The next day Samantha, one of my new friends, invited June and me to a party at her house for next Friday too. She also specifically told me that Jessica was not invited. Before I knew it, I was telling her that I would love to come. As soon as the words rushed out of my mouth, I wanted to take them back, but I was too scared to tell her that I already had plans with Jessica. I knew she would ask what we were doing, and when I told her that we were eating pizza and watching a movie, she would say that was boring. She might even think I was boring like Jessica. I didn't want to lose her friendship. She was so much fun and knew everyone in the school. She had an older brother, Mario, who was very popular, and made it known to everyone that she was his little sister. I was finally popular, and it was because I was friends with Samantha. I couldn't lose her friendship, so I kept my mouth shut. I had been keeping it shut for a week. Both Jessica and Samantha thought I was coming to their houses the next day. And I had no idea what to do.

The next morning, as soon as I got to school, June ran up to me. "So, where are you going tonight, Claudette?" she asked.

"I am still not sure."

"Well, you have only a few hours to figure it out."

"I know, I know. Stop pressuring me. I'll figure it out."

Before I knew it, Samantha was walking up to us. "Hi, girls!" she shouted. "Can't wait until later, right?"

"Absolutely!" I quickly answered back.

At that moment Jessica appeared from nowhere next to me. "What's going on later?" she asked.

"Nothing you need to worry about," snapped Samantha.

I knew Samantha didn't care for Jessica, but there was no need for her to be that rude to her. I was just about to tell her how I felt, when I heard Jessica begin to say something to me as if she didn't even hear the comment.

"So, Claudette, you said you're bringing the popcorn tonight, right?"

Just then Samantha's head snapped around so fast, I thought she might get whiplash. I looked at Samantha, and she had an angry, puzzled look on her face. It was the kind of look she got when she didn't get her way. Then I looked at Jessica. She seemed to be so excited about getting together tonight.

"Actually Claudette has something better to do tonight," replied Samantha with her teeth clenched tightly.

"No, I don't," I responded. "I am hanging out with Jessica tonight."

Samantha looked at the both of us in amazement, and then marched away. I don't know where it came from, but I knew the right thing to do was to stick by my best friend, no matter what the consequences were.

Open-ended Question

Think about how Claudette changes from the beginning of the story until the end.

■ Explain how her attitude toward being friends with Samantha changes.

■ How do you think Claudette will feel about being popular from now on?

Use specific information from the passage and your own knowledge to support your answer.

Here is a sample answer to the question. Read the answer and decide what score you would give the response. Use the 4-point rubric in the appendix to help you.

> I think Claudette went from really wanting to be friends with Samantha to not caring if she was friends with Samantha. In one part of the story Claudette says, "I was finally popular, and it was because I was friends with Samantha." This showed how important it was for her to be friends with Samantha. Then later on in the story she said, "I knew Samantha didn't care for Jessica, but there was no need for her to be that rude to her." She even decided to go to Jessica's house instead of Samantha's house. That tells that she didn't care as much about being Samantha's friend.

What did you score this response? What was good about it? The student did answer the first part of the question. There are two quotes from the story to support that answer. The student even used quotation marks to let the reader know that the quote was taken directly from the passage. However, did you notice that the student did not answer both parts of the question? Also, the student did not restate the question. Therefore, this response would probably receive a score of 2, since it was not complete. The answer has been rewritten to completely answer the question. The changes that were made are in bold.

Claudette's attitude toward being friends with Samantha changes from really wanting to be friends with Samantha to not caring if she was friends with Samantha. In one part of the story Claudette says, "I was finally popular, and it was because I was friends with Samantha." This shows how important it was for her to be friends with Samantha. Then later on in the story she says, "I knew Samantha didn't care for Jessica, but there was no need for her to be that rude to her." She even decides to go to Jessica's house instead of Samantha's house. That tells that she doesn't care as much about being Samantha's friend.

Claudette will still want to be popular, but not if it means hurting her best friend. She says in the story, "I don't know where it came from, but I knew the right thing to do was to stick by my best friend, no matter what the consequences were." This shows how important it is for Claudette to stick by Jessica. Sticking by a friend is more important than being popular.

Now read the following passage and answer the question on the lines provided.

Granny Shows Reddy a Trick

(Taken from *The Adventures of Reddy Fox*,
by Thornton W. Burgess)

Every day Granny Fox led Reddy Fox over to the long railroad bridge and made him run back and forth across it until he had no fear of it whatsoever. At first it had made him dizzy, but now he could run across at the top of his speed and not mind it in the least. "I don't see what good it does to be able to run across a bridge; anyone can do that!" exclaimed Reddy one day.

Granny Fox smiled. "Do you remember the first time you tried to do it?" she asked.

Reddy hung his head. Of course he remembered—remembered that Granny had had to scare him into crossing that first time.

Suddenly Granny Fox lifted her head. "Hark!" she exclaimed.

Reddy pricked up his sharp, pointed ears. Way off back, in the direction from which they had come, they heard the baying of a dog. It wasn't the voice of Bowser the Hound but of a younger dog. Granny listened for a few minutes. The voice of the dog grew louder as it drew nearer.

"He certainly is following our track," said Granny Fox. "Now, Reddy, you run across the bridge and watch from the top of the little hill over there. Perhaps I can show you 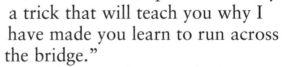 a trick that will teach you why I have made you learn to run across the bridge."

Reddy trotted across the long bridge and up to the top of the hill, as Granny had told him to. Then he sat down to watch. Granny trotted out in the middle of a field and sat down. Pretty soon a young hound broke out of the bushes, his nose in Granny's track. Then he looked up and saw her, and his voice grew still more savage and eager. Granny Fox started to run as soon as she was sure that the hound had seen her, but she did not run very fast. Reddy did not know what to make of it, for Granny seemed simply to be playing with the hound and not really trying to get away from him at all. Pretty soon Reddy heard another sound. It was a long, low rumble. Then there was a distant whistle. It was a train.

Granny heard it, too. As she ran, she began to work back toward the long bridge. The train was in sight now. Suddenly Granny Fox started across the bridge so fast that she looked like a little red streak. The dog was close at her heels when she started and he was so eager to catch her that he didn't see either the bridge or the train. But he couldn't begin to run as fast as Granny Fox. Oh, my, no! When she had reached the other side, he wasn't halfway across, and right behind him, whistling for him to get out of the way, was the train.

The hound gave one frightened yelp, and then he did the only thing he could do; he leaped down, down into the swift water below, and the last Reddy saw of him he was frantically trying to swim ashore.

"Now you know why I wanted you to learn to cross a bridge; it's a very nice way of getting rid of dogs," said Granny Fox, as she climbed up beside Reddy.

Open-ended Question

Think about how Granny Fox gets rid of the young hound dog.

- ▪ What is one word that you would use to describe Granny? Explain your answer.

- ▪ How might Reddy's feelings about crossing the bridge have changed from the beginning of the story to the end?

Use specific information from the passage and your own knowledge to support your answer.

Write your response here.

_____

_____

_____

_____

_____

_____

_____

_____

_____

_____

_____

_____

_____

_____

_____

_____

_____

_____

_____

_____

_____

_____

_____

_____

_____

_____

_____

_____

_____

_____

_____

_____

_____

_____

_____

_____

_____

Time to Check:

Did you:

■ remember to use the ANSWER strategy?

■ write neatly?

Check the rubric and score yourself. Is there anywhere you can improve your response?

PICTURE AND SPECULATIVE PROMPTS

Another part of the NJ ASK is the picture or speculative prompt. The test may include either, or even both, of these types of writing assessments. Your job will be to look at the prompts and write a narrative based on them. A narrative is a story that you will be writing based on the prompt that you see or read. This chapter will guide you through the process of writing a narrative based on the prompt you are given.

In this chapter you will:

■ learn to write a narrative story based on a picture prompt

■ review sample picture prompts

■ learn how to respond to a speculative prompt

■ review sample speculative writing prompts

NARRATIVES BASED ON A PICTURE PROMPT

When you are given a picture prompt, your job is to write a story based on that picture. The picture should be a major scene in your story. Imagine that you have written a book and that picture is an illustration in your book. You will have approximately 25 minutes to complete this task. The first step in beginning the narrative is brainstorming, the same way you began the persuasive essay. You will be given a brainstorming page in your answer booklet right before the page where you need to do your writing. Use this page to get your ideas down before you begin to write.

Once you have your ideas organized, you can begin to write the narrative. There are some things to remember as you are writing your story. These tips are included in the chart. Make sure you include them so that you receive the highest score possible. The rubric that is used to score your writing will most likely be the same as the one used for the persuasive essay. The scores can range from a 1 to a 6. Of course, the goal is to try to receive a 6.

Tip	Explanation
■ Begin with a hook.	You want to begin your story in such a way that the reader will be interested from the beginning. There are several possible ways to begin. ■ Use dialogue between characters. ■ Include an interesting question. This question should not be answered with a yes or no. Instead, it should get the reader thinking about a certain topic. (See the example in Chapter 2, The Persuasive Essay.) ■ Begin with three interesting adjectives to describe a main character or the setting. (Example: Hot, sticky, and smothering was the air on this August morning.)
■ Include compositional risks. (Only include them if you are sure you are using them correctly.)	Examples of compositional risks are: ■ using figurative language ■ dialogue ■ complex sentences
■ Give your characters names.	Just calling your main characters he or she does not keep the reader's attention.

Tip	Explanation
■ Write a story that includes the picture as a main scene.	Don't just tell about what's happening in the picture. (Example: In this picture the lady is in her garden…) Instead, write a complete story. The picture should be a *main scene* in the story, and not just quickly mentioned.
■ Include conflict in the story.	Any good story has a conflict. Your story should be no exception. Remember to include a conflict and a resolution in your story. (Go back to Chapter 3 if you've forgotten about conflicts.)
■ Make sure your story has a good beginning, middle, and end.	Your story should be interesting throughout. In order to do this, include great descriptions, details, and a good ending. You don't want to bore your reader, and you definitely don't want to disappoint the reader with a rushed or dull ending.
■ Remember proper grammar, mechanics, and sentence structure.	Try your best to include end marks where they belong, commas if you need them, and correct spelling. Also, if your story is taking place in the past, use past tense verbs (jumped, ran, went). If it is taking place in the present, use present tense verbs (jump, run, go). Try to avoid using both. This can confuse the reader.

Tip	Explanation
▪ Write neatly.	You can have the greatest story ever, but if the evaluator cannot read it, your score will be very low.
▪ Stay within the lines provided.	You will be given two pages of lines on which to write your story. Any writing in the margins may not be counted, so make sure your writing is only on the lines.

SAMPLE PICTURE PROMPT

Look at the picture prompt to the right. Then read the narrative that goes with the picture. What score do you think the story deserves? Look at the 6-point rubric in the appendix to remind you of the requirements.

One day a grandaughter came to visit her grandfather. He told her she looked just like her mother with her hair in pigtales. The littel girl said really? She asked him what her mother looked like when she was little. He told her he would show her.

The grandfather told the granddaughter to come and look at some pictures on the couch. He opened the book and pointed to a littel girl in pigtales wearing a blue and white striped dress. The grandfather told the girl that it was a *picture of her mother when she was the littel girls age. The grandfather then told the granddaughter that her mother hated that dress, but her mother made her ware it that day. The granddaughter said just like my mother makes me ware things that I don't like! yes her grandfather said. They both started laughing so hard that the littel girl almost fell off the couch. Her grandfather caut her. Then they started laughing some more.*

This story would probably receive a score of 2. Did the author begin with an interesting hook? The hook probably could have been better. Also, there are many spelling and punctuation mistakes, which make parts of it difficult to read. The story does include what is in the picture, but there is no real conflict and resolution, and very few details. Also, the characters are not named, which does not help to keep the reader's interest.

RESPONDING TO A PICTURE PROMPT

Now it's your turn. Remember the tips in the chart as you write your narrative.

Writing Task

Take a look at the picture prompt to the right. Use the blank space to brainstorm first. Brainstorm for about 5 minutes in the pre-write/plan section, and then begin to write on the lines provided.

Pre-write/plan here:

Write your response here.

_____

_____

_____

_____

_____

_____

_____

_____

_____

_____

_____

_____

Time to Check:

Did you:

- remember to begin with a hook?

- write a quality story from beginning to end?

- stay within the lines?

- use your neatest handwriting and best grammar, spelling, and punctuation?

- include the picture as a main scene of your story?

How would you score your narrative? Is there anything you can do to improve your story? If so, go back and improve it now.

SPECULATIVE PROMPTS

Speculative prompts are situations that are given and involve some type of problem that must be solved. It is the student's responsibility to create a story based on the situation and make sure that the story includes a resolution. You should still use all of the tips for writing a story based on a picture prompt. The only difference is that this time you are writing a story based on a given situation (including a conflict), and not a picture. The speculative prompt response will also be scored by the 6-point rubric that we used earlier in the chapter.

SAMPLE SPECULATIVE PROMPT

Here is an example. Read the prompt and think about how you would respond to it. Then read the given narrative and see what score you think it deserves.

Prompt: An eighth grade girl was a great actress. She was the lead in the school play each year, and this year was no exception. During play practice she remembered every line perfectly. As soon as she stepped on stage, she suddenly forgot everything.

Jessica was perfect. She had the perfect face, perfect body, the perfect life. She was the girl that all of the others wanted to be like, not just because she was beautiful, but also because she was funny and very thoughtful. Jessica also had the lead in the big school play. Everyone was busy practicing there lines. Everyone except Jessica.

"Aren't you going to practice?" asked Ashley.

"Nope, I don't need to. I know my lines inside and out," replied Jessica.

"I know I know, but can you run through my lines with me?" said Ashley.

"Ok," said Jessica.

The two girls practiced Ashley's lines until it was time to go home to change for the big performance that night. They headed home and wished each other good luck. As Jessica walked home, she imagined what it would be like to be on stage with everyone watching. She had done that before, but never as an eighth grader. This was her last year to shine with her classmates. She couldn't wait!

It was finally time. The car ride from home back to school seemed to take forever. Jessica was so excited, she felt like her heart was going to beat right out of her chest. She could tell that her parents were proud of her by the way they kept smiling at each other, then at her. Everything seemed to be perfect!

She could hear the crowd talking as she stood on the stage behind the curtain. She then heard Mrs. Jones, there Drama teacher, tell everyone to get in place. Jessica took her position in the center of the stage. She was ready for the curtain to rise and for the play to begin. It was happening just as she had imagined it. The chorus began to sing and then it was her turn to speak. Jessica opened her mouth and her mind went blank. She stared into the audience like a deer in headlights.

"Jessica, what's wrong?" whispered Ashley from the side. "Mind's blank," Jessica said.

Jessica began to panic. Beads of sweat began to break out on her forehead. She told herself, "Calm down. Try to remember the lines on the paper." What was she going to do? It was like her brain decided to go home. The thought of running off of the stage and straight home kept racing though her mind. "No," thought Jessica, "I won't ruin my last performance here! Imagine the words on the paper. Imagine the words on the paper. Imagine..." Just then, the words came back to her! She went on with the play as if nothing had happened.

After it was all over, Jessica's brother, Jason came up to her. "What happened to you," he asked.

"I learned an important lesson," she said. "You can never be too prepared!"

What score would you give this response? This story would probably receive a score of 5. It includes the conflict and solves it. It also includes dialogue. Overall it is a good response to the prompt. However, there are some spelling errors, namely using *there* instead of *their*. Also, there is a paragraph that includes two characters speaking.

This should have been two separate paragraphs instead. Lastly, the writer used the word *said* too many times, instead of coming up with a more creative word. Try to avoid these problems when you write your response.

RESPONDING TO A SPECULATIVE PROMPT

Now it's your turn once again. Take a look at the speculative prompt. Use the blank space to brainstorm first. Brainstorm for about 5 minutes, and then begin to write on the lines provided. Remember to include a conflict in your narrative.

Writing Task

The grandmother couldn't wait for her grandchildren to arrive. They were coming to stay with her for the weekend. She decided to bake some chocolate-chip cookies, as a surprise for her grandchildren. She opened her refrigerator and got a surprise of her own!

■ Write a story about the grandmother, her surprise, and the outcome.

Pre-write/plan here:

Write your response here.

_____

_____

_____

_____

_____

_____

_____

_____

_____

_____

_____

_____

_____

_____

_____

_____

_____

_____

_____

_____

_____

_____

_____

_____

_____

_____

_____

_____

_____

_____

_____

_____

_____

_____

Time to Check:

Did you:

- remember to begin with a hook?

- write a quality story from beginning to end?

- stay within the lines?

- use your neatest handwriting and best grammar, spelling, and punctuation?

- include the conflict that was provided and create your own solution?

How would you score your narrative? Is there anything you can do to improve your story? If so, go back and improve it now.

Chapter 6

PRACTICE WHAT
YOU HAVE LEARNED

There are two practice tests in this chapter for you to complete. Make sure to answer all questions completely, and double-check your work when you finish. Remember to use the strategies you have learned in the earlier chapters of this book. Good luck!

PRACTICE TEST ONE

PART I: PICTURE PROMPT

You will have 25 minutes to look at the picture, brainstorm ideas, write a narrative, and then edit your story. Use the pre-writing/planning section to write down ideas, and then write your story on the lines provided. If you have time, remember to check your work when you have finished.

Directions: Every picture tells a story. Look closely at the picture. What is happening in the picture? Use your imagination and experience to tell what this story is about.

Pre-write/plan here:

Write your response here.

PART II: READING PASSAGE

In this part of the test, you will read a passage and then answer the multiple-choice and open-ended questions that follow. You will have 45 minutes to complete this task.

Casey at the Bat

by Ernest Thayer

The outlook wasn't brilliant for the Mudville nine that day;
The score stood four to two, with but one inning more
    to play,
And then when Cooney died at first, and Barrows did
    the same,
A pall-like silence fell upon the patrons of the game.

A straggling few got up to go in deep despair. The rest
Clung to that hope which springs eternal in the human breast;
They thought, "If only Casey could but get a whack
    at that —
We'd put up even money now, with Casey at the bat."

But Flynn preceded Casey, as did also Jimmy Blake,
And the former was a hoodoo, while the
    latter was a cake;
So upon that stricken multitude grim
    melancholy sat;
For there seemed but little chance of Casey
    getting to the bat.

But Flynn let drive a single, to the
    wonderment of all,
And Blake, the much despised, tore the
    cover off the ball;
And when the dust had lifted, and men
    saw what had occurred,
There was Jimmy safe at second
    and Flynn a-hugging third.

Then from five thousand throats and more there rose a
   lusty yell;
It rumbled through the valley, it rattled in the dell;
It pounded on the mountain and recoiled upon the flat,
For Casey, mighty Casey, was advancing to the bat.

There was ease in Casey's manner as he stepped into
   his place;
There was pride in Casey's bearing and a smile lit
   Casey's face.
And when, responding to the cheers, he lightly doffed
   his hat,
No stranger in the crowd could doubt 'twas Casey at
   the bat.

Ten thousand eyes were on him as he rubbed his hands
   with dirt.
Five thousand tongues applauded when he wiped them
   on his shirt.
Then while the writhing pitcher ground the ball into his hip,
Defiance flashed in Casey's eye, a sneer curled Casey's lip.

And now the leather-covered sphere came hurtling through
   the air,
And Casey stood a-watching it in haughty grandeur there.
Close by the sturdy batsman the ball unheeded sped —
"That ain't my style," said Casey. "Strike one!" the
   umpire said.

From the benches, black with people, there went up a
   muffled roar,
Like the beating of the storm-waves on a stern and
   distant shore;
"Kill him! Kill the umpire!" shouted someone on
   the stand;
And it's likely they'd have killed him had not Casey
   raised his hand.

With a smile of Christian charity great Casey's visage shone;
He stilled the rising tumult; he bade the game go on;
He signaled to the pitcher, and once more the dun
    sphere flew;
But Casey still ignored it, and the umpire said "Strike two!"

"Fraud!" cried the maddened thousands, and echo
    answered "Fraud!"
But one scornful look from Casey and the audience was awed.
They saw his face grow stern and cold, they saw his
    muscles strain,
And they knew that Casey wouldn't let that ball go by again.

The sneer has fled from Casey's lip, the teeth are clenched
    in hate;
He pounds with cruel violence his bat upon the plate.
And now the pitcher holds the ball, and now he lets it go,
And now the air is shattered by the force of Casey's blow.

Oh, somewhere in this favored land the sun is shining bright,
The band is playing somewhere, and somewhere hearts
    are light,
And somewhere men are laughing, and little children shout,
But there is no joy in Mudville — mighty Casey has
    struck out.

Directions: Circle the correct answer for each multiple-choice question. Then answer the open-ended questions on the lines provided.

1. "Tore the cover off the ball" is an example of:

   A. conflict.

   B. figurative language.

   C. mood.

   D. cause and effect.

2. In the eleventh stanza, the word *awed* most nearly means:

   A. intimidated.

   B. depressed.

   C. yelling.

   D. lazy.

3. Why is it important for Casey to come to bat?

   A. He will get the crowd to cheer.

   B. He will tire out the pitcher.

   C. He will yell at the umpire.

   D. He will win the game.

4. Casey can best be described as:

   A. confident.

   B. quiet.

   C. awful.

   D. shameful.

5. Which best describes the plot of the passage?

   A. The home team is winning, their best player comes to bat, and he hits a home run.

   B. The home team is winning, their best player comes to bat, and he strikes out.

   C. The home team is losing, their best player comes to bat, and he strikes out.

   D. The home team is losing, their worst player comes to bat, and he strikes out.

6. What is Casey's reaction to the crowd yelling at the umpire?

   A. He is proud.

   B. He yells right along with them.

   C. He looks at them and smiles.

   D. He looks at them so they will stop.

7. "Five thousand tongues applauded," most closely means

   A. people are cheering.

   B. people are clapping.

   C. people are silent.

   D. people are whistling.

8. Casey's teeth are clenched in hate because:

    A. he doesn't like the umpire.

    B. he is mad that he swung and missed.

    C. he doesn't like crowd booing.

    D. he doesn't like the pitcher.

9. In the third stanza, the word *melancholy* most nearly means:

    A. quiet.

    B. depressed.

    C. hopeful.

    D. surprised.

10. Which player in the passage is the first to reach base?

    A. Casey

    B. Blake

    C. Flynn

    D. Cooney

11. The hometown crowd can't wait for Casey to get up to bat. Think about how they are feeling during the game.

   ▪ How did the crowd's feelings change from the time Casey gets to bat until the end of the game?

   ▪ How might they treat Casey the next time he comes to bat in a game?

   Use information from the passage and your own experience to answer the question.

   _____

   _____

   _____

   _____

   _____

   _____

   _____

   _____

   _____

   _____

   _____

   _____

   _____

   _____

12. Everyone is hoping Casey will come to bat and win the game. Think about how Casey might feel.

▪ What does Casey expect to do when he comes to bat?

▪ How might Casey feel the next time he comes to bat?

Use information from the passage and your own experience to answer the question.

_____

_____

_____

_____

_____

_____

_____

_____

_____

_____

_____

_____

_____

_____

_____

_____

PART III: PERSUASIVE PROMPT

You will have 45 minutes to respond to the following prompt. You can brainstorm in the pre-writing/planning section, and then write your response on the lines provided.

Writing Task

The student council of your school has proposed that vending machines be put in the school so that students can get a snack or drink during lunch or after school. The principal is concerned about promoting unhealthy snacks and drinks in the school, so he/she has decided to wait to make a final decision about having the vending machines installed.

Directions: Write a letter to the principal telling how you feel about having vending machines installed in your school.

Pre-write/plan here:

Write your response here.

_____

_____

_____

_____

_____

_____

_____

_____

_____

_____

_____

_____

_____

_____

_____

_____

_____

_____

_____

_____

_____

ANSWERS TO PRACTICE TEST ONE

Part I: Sample Picture Prompt Response

"What's in this box?" Craig yelled from the basement.

"Your dad's old baseball equipment." replied his mom.

Craig was so excited that he grabbed the box and brought it up the stairs and into the back yard. Craig's best friend Kevin would be coming over any minute and Craig couldn't wait to show him his dad's old baseball stuff.

"Hey Craig" Kevin said as he walked into the back yard, "what's that?"

"My dad's old baseball stuff. Let's check it out." Craig answered.

The boys looked in the box and saw two old gloves, an old baseball, some pictures, and a uniform. They looked through everything and decided to use the gloves and baseball and play catch in the yard. The ball was thrown back and forth many times.

"Throw it really far" yelled Kevin.

"Ok, get ready" Craig yelled back.

Craig threw the ball over Kevin's head. It landed on the ground and kept rolling down the street. The ball rolled right into the sewer. The boys ran after it.

"Oh no!" shouted Craig.

"What do we do now?" asked Kevin.

The boys knew they had to admit what happened to Kevin's father. They slowly walked back up the street and into Craig's house. They found Craig's father in his office and told him what had happened. Then they expected the yelling to begin.

"I am glad you told me the truth," Craig's father said, "but it's not a big deal. It was just an old ball that was still in the box because I forgot to throw it out."

"Really? I thought it was a special baseball or something," Craig said.

"Wow, that worked out a lot better than I expected," stated Kevin.

"Tell me about it. I guess honesty is the way to go." Laughed Kevin.

This response would probably receive a score of 5.

Part II: Answers to Multiple-choice Questions

1. **B** Since the cover is not actually torn off the ball, this is an example of figurative language.

2. **A** The audience feels intimidated because they receive a scornful look from Casey and his face grows cold, showing that he is unhappy.

3. **D** The crowd is looking forward to Casey coming to bat. Since their team is behind, they think he will be able to win the game for them.

4. **A** He is confident because the story says he is full of pride and smiling.

5. **C** The other answer choices have at least one wrong part.

6. **D** The passage says that, after the crowd yells at the umpire, Casey gives a scornful look and the audience is awed, or surprised.

7. **A** Applauding usually involves clapping, but in this case, the word *tongues* is used. Therefore, the passage is talking about the crowd using their mouths to cheer.

8. **B** Casey expects to hit the ball. When he doesn't, he becomes angry and clenches his teeth.

9. **B** The word means "depressed." The crowd is depressed because it doesn't look like Casey is going to get to bat.

10. **C** Flynn gets a single, and then is on third base. Blake is at second base.

Sample Answers to Open-ended Questions

11. The crowd's reaction changed a lot from the time Casey got to bat until the end of the game. In the beginning, when Casey got to bat, they were happy and cheering. The story says that, "And when, responding to the cheers, he lightly doffed his hat." This proves that they were excited and looking forward to Casey winning the game for them. As the umpire called strikes on Casey, they were upset and started to boo the umpire. After Casey struck out and their team lost the game, they were very unhappy and upset. In fact the passage says that, "But there was no joy in Mudville— mighty Casey has struck out."

    Casey will probably still be cheered by the crowd the next time he comes to bat.

They loved him before he struck out, and will probably still love him. When I have gone to baseball games, and the best player strikes out, the next time he is up, the crowd still cheered for him. I think they will do the same for Casey. At one point in the story, "Five thousand tongues applauded." This means that many fans were cheering for him. I think they will still cheer, especially since he only struck out that one time.

This response would probably receive a score of 4.

12. Casey expected to get a hit and win the game for the team. As Casey came to bat, the passage said, 'There was ease in Casey's manner as he stepped into his place; There was pride in Casey's bearing and a smile lit Casey's face." This tells that he was confident that he would do his job. That job was to win the game.

The next time Casey comes to bat he might feel a bit worried. He was so sure that he would get a hit the last time and since he didn't, he might not be so sure of him self. He must have seen how the crowd was sad after he struck out. He will probably remember this when he comes to bat the next time and feel bad. I know when I struck out, the next time I came up to bat I was not as confident because I thought If I struck out last time, maybe I will strike out again this time. Casey might feel the same.

This response would probably receive a score of 3.

Part III: Sample Persuasive Essay Response

Dear Principal Smith,

It's 3:00, the bell rings to end the school day and students are making their way to the busses. They are exhausted from a long day of learning. Many of the students have hours of homework ahead of them, and some have practice too. What they really need is a quick snack to boost their energy. This is why vending machines are necessary in school.

First of all, vending machines are a handy way to get a snack. Many students go straight from school to baseball or football practice. There is no where else to get a snack for energy. There are so many times when the coach yells at players to put more effort into the practice. They can't do that because they don't have the energy.

Second, there are so many healthy snacks out there that can be put in the vending machines, like dried fruit. Several students do not like to eat healthy. They would rather choose junk food over healthy food. When students are hungry, they will eat anything. If the vending machines included healthy snacks and drinks, the hungry students would buy them and finally eat a healthy snack.

Third, the vending machines are a great way to raise money for the school. Most students would buy something from them every day. Think of all of the money that would be. The school could use so many things, like a new front sign. The money used from the vending machines could buy a new sign and so many other things that would benefit our school.

In conclusion, installing a new vending machine is important to our school. Students need energy after school. A vending machine could help this problem. It could be a handy place for students to get a snack, it could offer a selection of healthy snacks for students, and the money raised form the vending machine could help to pay for things for the school. Please think about these ideas and decide to have the vending machines installed in school.

Sincerely,

Mark B.

This response would probably receive a score of 6.

PRACTICE TEST TWO

PART I: SPECULATIVE PROMPT

You will have 25 minutes to read the prompt, brainstorm ideas, write, and then edit your story. Use the pre-writing/ planning section to write down your ideas, and then write your story on the lines provided.

Writing Task

The big game was finally here. The score was tied. The crowd was going crazy, cheering for the home team. All of a sudden the crowd fell silent.

Directions: Write a story about the game, why the crowd fell silent, and the outcome.

Pre-write/plan here:

Write your response here.

_____

_____

_____

_____

_____

_____

_____

_____

_____

_____

_____

_____

_____

_____

_____

_____

_____

_____

_____

_____

_____

_____

PART II: READING PASSAGE

In this part of the test, you will read a passage and then answer the multiple-choice and open-ended questions that follow. You will have 45 minutes to complete this task.

Iktomi and the Muskrat
A Dakota Legend

by Zitkala-Sa

BESIDE a white lake, beneath a large grown willow tree, sat Iktomi on the bare ground. The heap of smoldering ashes told of a recent open fire. With ankles crossed together around a pot of soup, Iktomi bent over some delicious boiled fish.

Fast he dipped his black horn spoon into the soup, for he was ravenous. Iktomi had no regular meal times. Often when he was hungry he went without food.

Well hid between the lake and the wild rice, he looked nowhere save into the pot of fish. Not knowing when the next meal would be, he meant to eat enough now to last some time.

"How, how, my friend!" said a voice out of the wild rice. Iktomi started. He almost choked with his soup. He peered through the long reeds from where he sat with his long horn spoon in mid-air.

"How, my friend!" said the voice again, this time close at his side. Iktomi turned and there stood a dripping muskrat who had just come out of the lake.

"Oh, it is my friend who startled me. I wondered if among the wild rice some spirit voice was talking. How, how, my friend!" said Iktomi. The muskrat stood smiling. On his lips hung a ready "Yes, my friend," when Iktomi would ask, "My friend, will you sit down beside me and share my food?"

That was the custom of the plains people. Yet Iktomi sat silent. He hummed an old dance-song and beat gently on the edge of the pot with his buffalo-horn spoon. The muskrat began to feel awkward before such lack of hospitality and wished himself under water.

After many heart throbs Iktomi stopped drumming with his horn ladle, and looking upward into the muskrat's face, he said:

"My friend, let us run a race to see who shall win this pot of fish. If I win, I shall not need to share it with you. If you win, you shall have half of it." Springing to his feet, Iktomi began at once to tighten the belt about his waist.

"My friend Ikto, I cannot run a race with you! I am not a swift runner, and you are nimble as a deer. We shall not run any race together," answered the hungry muskrat.

For a moment Iktomi stood with a hand on his long protruding chin. His eyes were fixed upon something in the air. The muskrat looked out of the corners of his eyes without moving his head. He watched the wily Iktomi concocting a plot.

"Yes, yes," said Iktomi, suddenly turning his gaze upon the unwelcome visitor, "I shall carry a large stone on my back. That will slacken my usual speed; and the race will be a fair one."

Saying this he laid a firm hand upon the muskrat's shoulder and started off along the edge of the lake. When they reached the opposite side Iktomi pried about in search of a heavy stone.

He found one half-buried in the shallow water. Pulling it out upon dry land, he wrapped it in his blanket.

"Now, my friend, you shall run on the left side of the lake, I on the other. The race is for the boiled fish in yonder kettle!" said Iktomi.

The muskrat helped to lift the heavy stone upon Iktomi's back. Then they parted. Each took a narrow path through the tall reeds fringing the shore. Iktomi found his load a heavy one. Perspiration hung like beads on his brow. His chest heaved hard and fast.

He looked across the lake to see how far the muskrat had gone, but nowhere did he see any sign of him. "Well, he is running low under the wild rice!" said he. Yet as he scanned the tall grasses on the lake shore, he saw not one stir as if to make way for the runner. "Ah, has he gone so fast ahead that the disturbed grasses in his trail have quieted again?" exclaimed Iktomi. With that thought he quickly dropped the heavy stone. "No more of this!" said he, patting his chest with both hands.

Off with a springing bound, he ran swiftly toward the goal. Tufts of reeds and grass fell flat under his feet. Hardly had they raised their heads when Iktomi was many paces gone.

Soon he reached the heap of cold ashes. Iktomi halted stiff as if he had struck an invisible cliff. His black eyes showed a ring of white about them as he stared at the empty ground. There was no pot of boiled fish! There was no water-man in sight! "Oh, if only I had shared my food like a real Dakota, I would not have lost it all! Why did I not know the muskrat would run through the water? He swims faster than I could ever run! That is what he has done. He has laughed at me for carrying a weight on my back while he shot hither like an arrow!"

Crying thus to himself, Iktomi stepped to the water's brink. He stooped forward with a hand on each bent knee and peeped far into the deep water.

"There!" he exclaimed, "I see you, my friend, sitting with your ankles wound around my little pot of fish! My friend, I am hungry. Give me a bone!"

"Ha! ha! ha!" laughed the water-man, the muskrat. The sound did not rise up out of the lake, for it came down from overhead. With his hands still on his knees, Iktomi turned his face upward into the great willow tree. Opening wide his mouth he begged, "My friend, my friend, give me a bone to gnaw!"

"Ha! ha!" laughed the muskrat, and leaning over the limb he sat upon, he let fall a small sharp bone which dropped right into Iktomi's throat. Iktomi almost choked to death before he could get it out. In the tree the muskrat sat laughing loud. "Next time, say to a visiting friend, 'Be seated beside me, my friend. Let me share with you my food.'"

Directions: Circle the correct answer for each multiple-choice question. Then answer the open-ended questions on the lines provided.

1. In the third paragraph, the word *save* is used to mean:

   A. except.

   B. safe.

   C. keep.

   D. rid.

2. Iktomi can best be described as:

   A. generous.

   B. clever.

   C. quiet.

   D. selfish.

3. "Perspiration hung like beads" is an example of:

   A. personification.

   B. metaphor.

   C. hyperbole.

   D. simile.

4. The theme of this story can best be described as:

   A. It is best to have a fair race.

   B. It is best to share with a friend.

   C. Make sure you always have enough food.

   D. Make sure your opponent doesn't cheat.

5. The muskrat in the story can best be described as:

   A. clever.

   B. hungry.

   C. selfish.

   D. mean.

6. Why is the muskrat able to win the race?

   A. The heavy stone Iktomi is carrying makes it possible for the muskrat to run faster.

   B. The muskrat runs through the water.

   C. The muskrat makes Iktomi choke on the fish bone.

   D. The muskrat climbs the tree.

7. In paragraph thirteen, the word *slacken* most nearly means:

   A. increase.

   B. help.

   C. change.

   D. reduce.

8. In the story, the purpose of the words "shot hither like an arrow":

   A. is to compare the muskrat's ability to run and an arrow.

   B. is to compare the muskrat and the shape of an arrowhead.

   C. is to tell about weapons in the story.

   D. is to show how dangerous the muskrat is.

9. How does the muskrat feel when Iktomi does not offer the food?

   A. happy

   B. understanding

   C. confused

   D. embarrassed

10. Which of the following is *not* something that Iktomi does or feels when the muskrat arrives?

   A. Iktomi is startled.

   B. Iktomi is quiet.

   C. Iktomi is welcoming.

   D. Iktomi hums.

11. It is the custom for the Dakota to invite friends to eat if they visit during dinner time.

   ▪ If this is the custom, why doesn't Iktomi offer some of his food to the muskrat?

   ▪ If the same thing happened again, what do you think Iktomi would do?

   Use information from the passage and your own experience to answer the question.

   _____

   _____

   _____

   _____

   _____

   _____

   _____

   _____

   _____

   _____

   _____

   _____

   _____

   _____

   _____

   _____

12. All Iktomi receives from the big pot of his dinner is a bone. Do you think the muskrat is justified in eating all of Iktomi's food?

Use information from the passage and your own experience to answer the question.

_____

_____

_____

_____

_____

_____

_____

_____

_____

_____

_____

_____

_____

_____

_____

_____

_____

_____

_____

PART III: PERSUASIVE PROMPT

You will have 45 minutes to respond to the following prompt. You can brainstorm in the pre-writing/planning section, and then write your response on the lines provided.

Writing Task

After the last school dance, three teenagers from your school spray painted the school sign. This was not the first negative event occurring after a dance. The principal has decided to ban school dances, stating that they have contributed to many inappropriate actions by students.

Directions: Write a letter to the principal telling him/her how you feel about this decision.

Pre-write/plan here:

Write your response here.

_____

_____

_____

_____

_____

_____

_____

_____

_____

_____

_____

_____

_____

_____

_____

_____

_____

_____

_____

_____

_____

_____

_____

_____

_____

ANSWERS TO PRACTICE TEST TWO

Part I: Sample Speculative Prompt Response

Cheering waving and excited, the home team crowd poured into the gymnasium. The big game against Hills was finally here. The home team Valley was undefeated this season and their rival Hills was the only thing stopping them from a perfect basketball season. It was the only thing everyone was talking about.

The game raced by as fast as a cheetah. Before everyone knew it, the final period of the game arrived and the score was tied at 48 points. Each fan was reacting to the pressure in a different way. Some were biting their nails and others were holding Valley signs. Most of the fans were screaming, Go Valley go!"

All of a sudden the crowd fell silent. The worst possible thing happened. Dave Johnston Valley's best player was own on the floor grabbing his rite knee.

"Get up!" the crowd began to yell. Some of the crowd still stood silently praying for Dave to be ok.

The teams doctor rushed out and kneeled next to Dave. He asked Dave something and Dave nodded. Then he and the coach helped Dave Johnston off of the court.

Everyone stood in the stands in shock. Suddenly Jared Smith the back up point guard ran onto the court. Jared was not the best player on the team but he was al they had. The next *play had everyone holding their breath. With three seconds to go the ball was passed to Jared. Everyone started yelling "Shoot for three!"*

That's exactly what Jared did. With a swoosh sound the ball passed thru the net. "Valley wins!" came over the loud speaker. The crowd went wild. Suddenly Jared Smith went from second rate player to hero.

This response would probably receive a score of 5.

Part II: Answers to Multiple-choice Questions

1. **A** The word *except* makes sense when it is inserted into the sentence in place of *save*. He looked nowhere *except* in the pot.

2. **D** He is selfish because the story says that he does not offer some of his food, even when it is the custom to do so. Instead, he wants it all for himself.

3. **D** This phrase uses the word *like* and compares perspiration and beads.

4. **B** The muskrat tells Iktomi that he should share his food next time. It is a lesson he needs to learn and is the theme of this story.

5. **A** The muskrat wins the race not because he is the fastest runner on land, but because he is clever, or smart enough, to realize that he can swim faster than Iktomi can run.

6. **B** Iktomi states, "Why did I not know that the muskrat would run through the water?"

7. **D** Carrying a large stone on his back would reduce or lessen Iktomi's chances of winning since the load would be heavy.

8. **A** The muskrat "shot hither like an arrow" in the race. This phrase compares the muskrat's running and an arrow.

9. **C** The muskrat is expecting to be offered food. When he isn't, he feels awkward, or confused.

10. **C** The only thing that Iktomi does NOT do is welcome the muskrat. The passage states that he does the other choices.

Sample Answers to Open-ended Questions

11. Iktomi didn't share with the muskrat because he was selfish. It says that he ravenous. This shows that he really wanted the meal more than being a good Dakota. It also said, "Iktomi had no regular meal times. Often he was hungry and went without food." There were other times when he had been hungry. He probably figured it was best to eat all of the food at that time, since who knows when he would have food again.

If the same thing happened again, I think Iktomi would share his food. He seemed to learn his lesson. Since he didn't share the meal with the muskrat, not only did he lose his food, but he also almost choked on the bone that he was given by the muskrat. Next time he will probably remember what happened to him and then offer the food to the visitor. When I was younger and wouldn't share my toys, my mom took them away from me. Since I didn't want them to get taken away again, the next time I made sure I shared with my friends. I think Iktomi will do the same.

This response would probably receive a score of 3.

12. The muskrat was right to take Iktomi's meal. It says that the Dakota custom is to share a meal with a friend. Therefore Iktomi should have shared the meal with muskrat. Since he didn't, the muskrat had the right to teach Iktomi a lesson.

This response would probably receive a score of 2.

Part III: Sample Persuasive Essay Response

Dear Principle,

The week of a school dance is exciting and fun. All every one talks about is what they are going to ware and what they are going to do at the dance. All of a sudden we find out that there will be no more dances because of a few bad kids. It's not fair! That's why we should still have school dances.

One reason we should have school dances is that at dances students dance and dancing is good exercise. Many students are overwait and need to lose wait. This could be one way for them to lose wait. If there are no dances then they will stay the same wait. This will not be good.

Another reason we should have school dances is to help us socialy. Middle school students are very social. We like to talk to each other all of the time. Dances give us a chance to talk to our friends that we don't always see. They also help us to talk to students we don't know very well. Not all of the students are in our classes, so at least we can talk to them at dances.

Finally there should be an investagation to see which kids actually spray painted the sign. Once you find them, they should pay for thesign to be fixed and they should be suspended. Why should the kids who didn't do anything be punished? If we acted right at the dance, we should still get to go to a dance. The kids who don't act right should not be allowed to go.

In conclusion we should have school dances. It will help students to exercise, all of us can get to know each other better and only the ones who did something wrong should be punished. Please investagate to see who really did the spray painting. I am sure students who have information will tell what they know. This way we can keep school dances.

Thank you,

Sara D.

This response would probably receive a score of 4.

APPENDIX

ANSWERS TO WARM-UP DRILLS

Warm-up Drill #1—The Notebook

1. The correct answer is B. The first place we meet the main character is when she screams out in English class. The other choices are settings of the story, but they are later locations in the story.

2. The correct answer is C. Maria yells out in class and gets her friends involved in her plan. This shows that she is not quiet. Also, Maria is not a mean character. Her goal is not to get even with Josephine, but only to get her notebook back. She also feels badly for blaming Josephine for stealing her notebook. Maria, the main character, is determined to get her notebook back and gets her friends involved in helping her. Another word for determined is *strong-minded*, and that is why C is the correct answer.

3. The correct answer is D. The problem the main character faces is that she cannot find her notebook. Choices A and C do not occur in the story. The main character's friends do want to help her find the notebook, and she does not have a fight with another character in this story. Choice B is incorrect because it is not a problem the character faces in the story; instead it is an event that happened in the story.

4. The correct answer to this question is **A**. The protagonist is the character that must solve a problem. Maria is the one that has a problem in the story. Janeece and Patty are Maria's friends. Josephine is the character that Maria blames for taking her notebook.

5. The correct answer is **B**. This is the part of the story where conflict begins to get resolved. After taking the notebook from Josephine, Maria realizes that she is wrong for accusing Josephine of stealing her notebook. The other answers are events in the story, but they are not part of the climax.

6. The correct answer is **A**. Choices B and C are incorrect because at the end of the story, Josephine walks away from Maria. It never says whether or not they become friends. Choice D is incorrect because the story never tells us that Maria yells back at Josephine when Josephine accuses Maria of writing about her in Maria's journal.

7. The correct answer is **D**. Maria's problem is solved when Patty gives her back her notebook, and then tells Maria that she must have dropped it in the hallway. Choice A is incorrect because even though Maria wants to apologize to Josephine, she doesn't actually do it in the story. Choice B is incorrect because it does not happen in the passage. Choice C is wrong because Janeece finds a notebook in the locker, but it turns out to be the wrong one.

8. The correct answer to the question is **C**. Readers can learn from Maria that assuming can cause problems. Maria assumes that Josephine stole her notebook because of something Josephine had said earlier. Maria is proven wrong and then realizes she has to apologize to Josephine for what she did. Choices A and B are not really lessons the reader can learn from the story. Choice D is incorrect. Maria states that Mr. Klein is upset with her for yelling out in class.

9. The correct answer is D, identity. The notebook contains Maria's innermost thoughts and feelings that she doesn't want to share with others. They are what make her unique and an individual.

10. The correct answer is A. Maria, the main character, is telling the story. Sentences like, "Just then we saw Josephine walking toward hers," and "I ducked around the corner," show that the main character is telling the reader the story. The words *I* and *we* are used.

Warm-up Drill #2—Baby-sitting

1. The correct answer is C. This statement, "she knew that the card said he loved her," is the only statement that has an object acting like a human. In this case the card speaks. The other sentences involve only a human character.

2. The correct answer is B. The statement is not an exaggeration for effect, plus it is talking about a human. Therefore, choices A and D are incorrect. The statement is making a comparison between the brother and lightning. There is no use of *like* or *as*, so it cannot be a simile. Therefore, the statement is an example of a metaphor.

3. The correct answer is B. This simile compares Matty and a cheetah, an animal that moves very quickly. It helps us to understand how Matty moves. Therefore, choices C and D are not correct, since they are talking about something else. Choices A and B both concentrate on Matty's movements, but only B concentrates on how quickly he moves, and that is why B is correct.

4. The correct answer is A. Chances are Jamie hasn't actually baby-sat a million times before. She says this to demonstrate to her mother that she has done this many times already, and that she is annoyed that her mother is telling her information she already knows from baby-sitting before.

5. The correct answer is C. The author is telling the story. The only time the reader sees the word *I* used is when a character is speaking and the word *I* is part of a sentence that is in quotation marks.

Warm-up Drill #3—Trenton

1. The correct answer is C. The other answers tell more about Trenton's interesting history, so they are details. The entire paragraph tells about Trenton's history, so choice C is the main idea.

2. The correct answer is A. Trenton was so important that it became the capital of the United States. If it was minor, it probably would not have been named the capital, so choice C is incorrect. Choices B and D do not fit correctly into the meaning of the paragraph. A violent or big town probably would not become the capital of the United States.

3. The correct answer is B. If you read the paragraph carefully, the author does share feelings about Trenton with the reader. The author first says that Trenton has an interesting history. Then, the author says that Trenton was so significant that it became the capital of the United States. The author feels Trenton was important enough to be the country's capital. These two statements give a clue as to the author's opinion of Trenton.

4. The correct answer is B. The other choices tell about Trenton's history, which is the main idea. Washington may have won more battles, but this fact doesn't tell more about the main idea.

Warm-up Drill #4—A Home for the Mets

1. The correct answer is C. The reader is told that the new stadium is opening in the spring of 2009. The reader is also told that this new stadium is where the Mets will be playing. Therefore, we can infer that the Mets will no longer be playing in Shea Stadium after the opening of Citi Field. Choice A is a true statement, but the author clearly tells the reader that information. It doesn't have to be inferred, so it is not the correct choice. Choice B is wrong because the reader cannot assume that twice the number of fans will now go to a Mets game based on the information that is given. Choice D is an incorrect statement. The author tells us that Mets fans will not have to travel further to the new stadium.

2. The correct answer is A. The passage tells us that, because of the open view from the concession stands, the fans will still be able to see the game. The other choices may be facts, but they are not caused by the open view from the concession stands.

3. The correct answer is A. The paragraph tells how the two ballparks are alike, and therefore it is comparing them. It is not stating how they are different, which is why choice B is incorrect. Choices C and D are incorrect because, although food and grass are mentioned in the paragraph, both topics are not explained in detail.

4. The correct answer is D. We do not know if the new fans will applaud the new stadium. This is the author's opinion. The other choices are incorrect because they are facts.

ANSWERS TO SAMPLE PASSAGES

Warm-up Drill #5—The Rainout

1. **B** The phrase compares the boy and a bird, and it uses the work *like*.

2. **D** The sound comes immediately after the lightning, as thunder often does.

3. **A** He stomps up the stairs and slams the door shut, a sign he is angry.

4. **A** The character often uses the word *I* and is speaking to the reader.

5. **C** The other options aren't mentioned.

6. **A** *Never, ever* is an exaggeration.

7. **B** No other options are stated in the story.

8. **B** The other choices have at least one event that does not happen in the story.

9. **A** Billy has to accept not going to the game as a result of not trying his hardest.

10. **D** The rain gives Billy another chance (or opportunity) to see the game.

Warm-up Drill #6—Famous "New Jerseyans"

1. **C** The paragraph tells about both astronauts, not just one.

2. **B** The passage states that she carried pitchers, so we can infer that is how she got her nickname.

3. **A** The name of the band is not important in a passage about famous people from New Jersey.

4. **A** It is the only positive word that makes sense in the sentence.

5. **D** It cannot be proven that Frank Sinatra was one of the best singers of all time.

6. **B** The passage is about famous people from New Jersey.

7. **C** He is well known and captain of his team, a sign that he is admired.

8. **A** The passage talks about many famous people with different careers.

WRITING NEW JERSEY HOLISTIC SCORING RUBRIC–GRADES 6 AND 7

In scoring, consider the grid of written language	Inadequate Command	Limited Command	Partial Command	Adequate Command	Strong Command	Superior Command
Score	1	2	3	4	5	6
Content & Organization	• May lack opening and/or closing • Minimal response to topic; uncertain focus • No planning evident; disorganized • Details random, inappropriate, or barely apparent	• May lack opening and/or closing • Attempts to focus • May drift or shift focus • Attempts organization • Few, if any, transitions between ideas • Details lack elaboration that could highlight paper	• May lack opening and/or closing • Usually has single focus • Some lapses or flaws in organization • May lack some transitions between ideas • Repetitious details • Several unelaborated details	• Generally has opening and/or closing • Single focus • Ideas loosely connected • Transition evident • Uneven development of details	• Opening and closing • Single focus • Sense of unity and coherence • Key ideas developed • Logical progression of ideas • Moderately fluent • Attempts compositional risks • Details appropriate and varied	• Opening and closing • Single focus • Unified and coherent • Well-developed • Logical progession of ideas • Fluent, cohesive • Composi-tional risks successful • Details effective, vivid, explicit, and/or pertinent
Usage	• No apparent control • Severe/numerous errors	• Numerous errors	• Errors/patterns of errors may be evident	• Some errors that do not interfere with meaning	• Few errors	• Very few, if any, errors
Sentence Construction	• Assortment of incomplete and/or incorrect sentences	• Excessive monotony/same structure • Numerous errors	• Little variety in syntax • Some errors	• Some errors that do not interfere with meaning	• Few errors	• Very few, if any, errors
Mechanics	• Errors so severe they detract from meaning	• Numerous serious errors	• Patterns of errors evident	• No consistent pattern of errors • Some errors that do not interfere with meaning	• Few errors	• Very few, if any, errors
Nonscorable Responses	NR = No Response OT = Off Topic/Off Task NE = Not English WF = Wrong Format	Student wrote too little to allow reliable judgment of his/her writing. Student did not write on the assigned topic/task, or the student attempted to copy the prompt. Student wrote in a language other than English. Student refused to write on the topic, or the writing task folder was blank.				

Copyright New Jersey Department of Education. Reprinted with permission.

OPEN-ENDED SCORING RUBRIC FOR READING, LISTENING, AND VIEWING

Points	Criteria
4	A 4-point response clearly demonstrates understanding of the task, completes all requirements, and provides an insightful explanation/opinion that links to or extends aspects of the text.
3	A 3-point response demonstrates an understanding of the task, completes all requirements, and provides some explanation/opinion using situations or ideas from the text as support.
2	A 2-point response may address all of the requirements, but demonstrates a partial understanding of the task, and uses text incorrectly or with limited success resulting in an inconsistent or flawed explanation.
1	A l-point response demonstrates minimal understanding of the task, does not complete the requirements, and provides only a vague reference to or no use of the text.
0	A 0-point response is irrelevant or off-topic.

**New Jersey
Assessment
of Skills and
Knowledge 2006**

Writer's Checklist

Important Points to Remember as You Write

CONTENT/ORGANIZATION

_____ 1. Focus on your purpose for writing and your audience.

_____ 2. Develop a clear topic or central idea.

_____ 3. Support your ideas with details, explanations, and examples.

_____ 4. Put your ideas in the order that best communicates what you are trying to say.

SENTENCE CONSTRUCTION

_____ 5. Use clear and varied sentences.

USAGE

_____ 6. Use words correctly.

_____ 7. Use varied and vivid vocabulary.

MECHANICS

_____ 8. Capitalize, spell, and punctuate correctly.

_____ 9. Write neatly.

NEW JERSEY STATE DEPARTMENT OF EDUCATION

INDEX

Really. This isn't going to hurt at all . . .

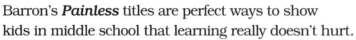

BARRON'S

Barron's *Painless* titles are perfect ways to show
kids in middle school that learning really doesn't hurt.
They'll even discover that grammar, algebra, and other subjects
that many of them consider boring can become fascinating—and yes, even fun!
The trick is in the presentation: clear instruction, taking details one step at a
time, adding a light and humorous touch, and sprinkling in some brain-tickler
puzzles that are both challenging and entertaining to solve.

Each book: Paperback, approx. 224 pp.

Painless Algebra, 2nd Ed.
Lynette Long, Ph.D.
ISBN 978-0-7641-3434-0

Painless American Government
Jeffrey Strausser
ISBN 978-0-7641-2601-7

Painless American History
Curt Lader
ISBN 978-0-7641-0620-0

**Painless English for Speakers of
Other Languages**
Jeffrey Strausser and José Paniza
ISBN 978-0-7641-3562-0

Painless Fractions, 2nd Ed.
Alyece Cummings
ISBN 978-0-7641-3439-5

Painless French
Carol Chaitkin and Lynn Gore
ISBN 978-0-7641-3735-8

Painless Geometry
Lynette Long, Ph.D.
ISBN 978-0-7641-1773-2

Painless Grammar, 2nd Ed.
Rebecca S. Elliott, Ph.D.
ISBN 978-0-7641-3436-4

Painless Italian
Marcel Danesi, Ph.D.
ISBN 978-0-7641-3630-6

Painless Math Word Problems
Marcie Abramson, B.S., Ed.M.
ISBN 978-0-7641-1533-2

Painless Poetry
Mary Elizabeth
ISBN 978-0-7641-1614-8

Painless Reading Comprehension
Darolyn E. Jones
ISBN 978-0-7641-2766-3

Painless Spanish
Carlos B. Vega
ISBN 978-0-7641-3233-9

Painless Speaking
Mary Elizabeth
ISBN 978-0-7641-2147-0

Painless Spelling, 2nd Ed.
Mary Elizabeth
ISBN 978-0-7641-3435-7

Painless Vocabulary
Michael Greenberg
ISBN 978-0-7641-3240-7

Painless Writing
Jeffrey Strausser
ISBN 978-0-7641-1810-4

Barron's Educational Series, Inc.
250 Wireless Boulevard, Hauppauge, NY 11788
In Canada: Georgetown Book Warehouse
34 Armstrong Avenue, Georgetown, Ont. L7G 4R9

Please visit **www.barronseduc.com**
to view current prices and to order books

(#79) R7/08

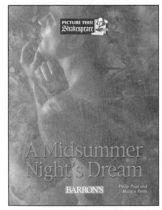
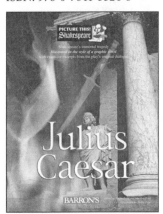

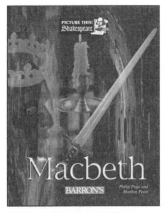

BARRON'S NEW JERSEY ASK6 MATH TEST

Mary Serpico, M.A.

This manual reviews the sixth grade math curriculum for the required New Jersey State math assessment test. Five subject review chapters cover the following topics: number and numerical operations; geometry and measurement; patterns and algebra; data analysis, probability, and discrete mathematics; and integrating the strands through mathematical processes. Two full-length practice tests are included with answers.

Paperback, 288 pp., ISBN 978-0-7641-3922-2

BARRON'S NEW JERSEY ASK6 LANGUAGE ARTS LITERACY TEST

Mary Beth Byrouty, M.Ed.

This brand-new manual offers solid preparation to sixth graders throughout the state of New Jersey as they get ready to take the required ASK Language Arts Literacy Test. It provides two full-length practice tests with answers and explanations, plus practice and review in all of the following test topics: reading and understanding passages, answering multiple-choice and open-ended questions, and writing a persuasive essay.

Paperback, 288 pp., ISBN 978-0-7641-3942-0

BARRON'S NEW JERSEY ASK7 MATH TEST

John Neral

Seventh graders preparing to take the New Jersey ASK math test will find a detailed review of all relevant math topics in this brand-new manual. Topics include integers, fractions, decimals, whole numbers and exponents, ratio and proportion, solving algebraic equations, patterns in algebra, pattern problems, inequalities, and much more. Each chapter includes practice and review questions with answers. Also included are two full-length practice tests with answers.

Paperback, 288 pp., ISBN 978-0-7641-3943-7

BARRON'S NEW JERSEY ASK7 LANGUAGE ARTS LITERACY TEST

Joseph S. Pizzo

This brand-new title reviews all topics covered on the statewide New Jersey Language Arts Literacy Test for seventh graders. Separate chapters instruct on writing a persuasive essay, reading and understanding literary forms, reading for information, and applying rules of grammar and style for effective writing. The book also presents two full-length practice tests with answers and explanations, strategies for test-taking success, and more.

Paperback, 288 pp., ISBN 978-0-7641-4019-8

BARRON'S NEW JERSEY ASK8 SCIENCE TEST

Jackie Halaw

This brand-new manual prepares eighth graders throughout New Jersey to succeed on the required statewide science test. The author opens with a general overview of science—its purposes and methodology, its terminology, its close connection with mathematics, and its many different branches. Chapters that follow present introductions to the various sciences, from biology and ecology to physics and astronomy. Practice questions in every chapter help students measure their learning progress. The book concludes with two full-length practice tests with questions answered and explained.

Paperback, 288 pp., ISBN 978-0-7641-4028-0

Barron's Educational Series, Inc.
250 Wireless Blvd.
Hauppauge, NY 11788
Order toll-free: 1-800-645-3476
Order by fax: 1-631-434-3723
In Canada:
Georgetown Book Warehouse
34 Armstrong Ave.
Georgetown, Ont. L7G 4R9
Canadian orders: 1-800-247-7160
Fax in Canada: 1-800-887-1594

Please visit www.barronseduc.com
to view current prices and to order books

BARRON'S

(#169) R 8/08